MARCH OF T

FROM SARGON II TO THE FALL OF NINEVEH

CAM REA

REA PUBLISHING

Cover design provided by Vikki at
http://fiverr.com/vikncharlie

Dedication

To my family

Acknowledgments

While I have been occupied with college for the last three years, I have been slowly researching and putting this book together, a task in and of itself when considering the amount of reading and papers one has to write during college on top of writing a book.

First, I would like to thank the Military History department at the American Military University for their help, but more importantly their encouragement. Secondly, I would like to thank my wife and our two beautiful sons for putting up with my odd hours and coffee sessions. Many hours, days, weeks, months, and years have gone into this book, all of which I hope you, the reader, will enjoy. Thirdly, I would like to thank Brett Schlotterback for his help in keeping my computer running. Lastly, I would like to thank Joan Griffith for taking the time to read, edit, read, and edit. Without her this book might have taken much longer to publish; she is a gem; and I am greatly appreciative of her input and guidance during this project.

CONTENTS

INTRODUCTION 1

1 MILITARY BYPRODUCT 5
    ASSYRIAN ARMY AUXILIARIES.. 10
    ENDNOTES: CHAPTER ONE.. 12

2 SARGON'S BLOWBACK..13
    CIMMERIAN REBELLION 22
    ENDNOTES: CHAPTER TWO..31

3 ESARHADDON'S CURSE...33
    ESARHADDON'S NORTHERN TROUBLE....................................35
    TEUSHPA..38
    ISHPAKA..41
    BARTATUA 45
    SCYTHIANS, KASTARITI AND THE COALITION 48
    CONCLUSION TO ESARHADDON..62
    ENDNOTES: CHAPTER THREE 64

4 ASHURBANIPAL'S HELL..67
    DUGDAMMI: KING OF THE WORLD..78
    MADYES, CYAXARES, AND AN ALTERNATIVE 98
    THE FALL OF ASSYRIA... 111
    WERE THE SCYTHIANS INVOLVED WITH THE FALL OF NINEVEH?.. 118
    ENDNOTES: CHAPTER FOUR...121

5 CONCLUSION... 127

APPENDIX I ARMS AND ARMOR...................................131
    BODY ARMOR..132
    HELMET...138

  Weapons 143
  Axe 143
  Lance 145
  Javelin 148
  Sword 149
  The Bow and Arrow 156
  Endnotes: Appendix I 169

APPENDIX II TACTICS 174

  Swarming 176
  Feinting 179
  Defense in Depth 181
  Endnotes: Appendix II 184

BIBLIOGRAPHY 185

INDEX 211

FIGURES

Figure 1 Neo-Assyrian Empire 27
Figure 2 History of the eighth campaign of Sargon II, king of Assyria, against Urartu. 714 BC, found in Assur 28
Figure 3 Lake Urmia 29
Figure 4 Manna 30
Figure 5 Armored Scythian Cavalryman 137
Figure 6 Parthian Horse Archers 138
Figure 7 Soft Pointed Caps 141
Figure 8 Assyrian wearing conical helmet 142
Figure 9 Scythian with sagaris in right hand 144
Figure 10 Parthian horsemen carrying a lance or javelin 147
Figure 11 Mithra holding an Akinakes 153
Figure 12 Darius the Great holding an Akinakes in left hand 154
Figure 13 Cimmerians 155
Figure 15 Scythian stringing his bow on the right 158
Figure 17 Scythian Archers 165
Figure 17 Scythian Trilobate Arrowheads courtesy of Sergi from Metal Detecting World.com 166

Introduction

The Cimmerians and the Scythians were nomadic peoples whose origin is uncertain. Many scholars in the fields of history, archaeology, Assyriology, and other disciplines disagree about their origin. Some argue the Cimmerians and Scythians came from the Black Sea region. Other historians argue that the Scythians came from Central Asia or that both the Cimmerians and Scythians re of Iranian origin. Moreover, others argue that the Cimmerians and Scythians are exiled Israelites who were deported following the Assyrian invasion of the Northern Kingdom of Israel in the eighth century BCE.

In any case, their origin is not important to the propositions presented here. Instead, this book focuses on the battle inscriptions left by Assyrians and a few left by Greeks who dealt with these nomadic peoples.

The first and second section of the book addresses their earlier history when Assyrian sources first mentioned them during the reign of Sargon II. It examines their effect on the Battle on Mt. Uaush in 714 BCE and its aftermath. It discusses why they rebelled against Sargon II, which led to his death.

The third section of the book examines King Esarhaddon of Assyria and his on-and-off fight with the

Scythians and Cimmerians and the many chieftains who challenged Assyria during his reign.

The fourth section of the book discusses the reign of Ashurbanipal and how he dealt with the Scythians and Cimmerians. In addition, it discusses Ashurbanipal's nervousness when a Cimmerian-Scythian king named Dugdammi threatened the Assyrian Empire. Because of Dugdammi's power, Ashurbanipal may have sent a Scythian chieftain named Madyes against Dugdammi to rid Assyria of its problem.

Other topics in this book are the story of Cyaxares and the account found in *The Fall of Nineveh Chronicle.* In addition, this book examines Herodotus' book, *The Histories,* in order to understand Cyaxares' role in the fall of Assyria and whether or not Scythians and Cimmerians were present by providing an alternative to the Cyaxares story.

Appendix I examines the arms and armor of the Cimmerians and Scythians. It discusses the many weapons used and touches upon the use of biological weapons. The purpose is to help the reader gain an understanding of their methodology in weaponry.

Appendix II focuses on Scythian and Cimmerian battle tactics, such as swarming and feinting. It discusses their defensive tactics in depth by revisiting some of the accounts of such historians as Herodotus and Plutarch.

The book focuses on inscriptions, the ancient historians' writings about the Scythians and Cimmerians, and the causes that led to the many battles against them. It also addresses how the Scythians and Cimmerians blended among the ranks of those who ruled them in times of war and peace.

I hope you enjoy this book and gain as much from it as I enjoyed writing it.

1

Military Byproduct

The first mention of the Cimmerians is in Assyrian inscriptions around 714 BCE during the reign of King Sargon II of Assyria. It is in 714 BCE that the Cimmerians were assisting Sargon in his campaign against the Kingdom of Urartu. The descriptions of the Cimmerians found in the Assyrian inscriptions suggest they are serving as auxiliary units. The inscriptions dealing with this event are very detailed, but not detailed as to the military aspects pertaining to the Cimmerians, such as what type of horse they rode and the kinds of weapons utilized. However, we are not at a complete loss. We shall look to the Assyrian war machine to get a better idea of how the Cimmerian and Scythian tribes served under the Assyrian military umbrella.

The Assyrians were the first to standardize a true and professional cavalry unit during the reign of Tiglath-pileser III of Assyria. Before then, the Assyrians relied on cavalry teams. This consisted of a charioteer riding one horse and holding the reins of the other horse, leaving the other charioteer archer free to shoot the enemy with arrows as they rode around. This method was about to change.

Tiglath-pileser III invaded the province of Media, east of Assyria, in the 8th century BCE and noticed the Median cavalry's effectiveness in combat.[1] Reliefs during the reign of Ashurbanipal II in the 9th century BCE depict the Assyrians as already having small units of light cavalry. Their only function was to ward off other horse archer units during engagements. What the Assyrians did was take regular foot archers and place them on horseback. The Assyrians now had their own version of a horse archer, but they wore little or no armor. This made the Assyrian horse archer vulnerable to attacks from other horse archers who were better armored and trained in the art of archery from horseback. Tiglath-pileser took note of what could be adopted to improve his own cavalry.[2] Tiglath-pileser would invest a good amount in developing better cavalry units,[3] whereas his later enemies, the Cimmerians and Scythians, would continue to evolve into a much better fighting force that adapted to the natural conditions and the method of war conducted by their enemies. In other words, improvise, adapt, and overcome.

The Assyrians also employed nomadic cavalry units to do much of their fighting for them. Even though Assyria did incorporate and adopt the cavalry style of those living on the Iranian plateau they looked to those cultures that primarily used cavalry to fight alongside them.[4] The Assyrians not only aimed to train themselves in the rudimentary art of horsemanship, they also taught the deportees assigned to the regions where cavalry was needed most. Some deportees were prized for their understanding of horsemanship, for they could be quickly placed in a region or district to defend Assyria's borders, like Gamri, where the Cimmerians are first mentioned in Assyrian text, where the terrain was not suited for chariot warfare due to its mountainous features.[5]

After conquering a portion of western Media, Tiglath-pileser incorporated Median cavalry into his own army, effectively changing the nature of the Assyrian cavalry from charioteer teams to mounted warriors armed with bow and spear. The days of the chariot as master of the battlefield were nearing an end. Over time, the Assyrian military would have three types of cavalry. The first type is light cavalry, which is quick, nimble, and speedy, consisting of Medes and other nomads. Their primary weapons were the bow and javelin. Next came the Assyrian heavy horse archers, men in heavy scaled body armor. Due to their armor, they likely confronted other horse archers and infantry at close range. Last, we have the heavy cavalryman, meant to engage heavy infantry and cavalry. Tiglath-pileser and his successors loved the new cavalry system so much that they would replace most of the chariot units with elite cavalry units over time. To put this into perspective, the king, his nobles, and the warrior elite became the only ones permitted to use the chariot.[6]

In order to supply the cavalry, the Assyrians would request the provision of 3,000 horses each month. The horse recruitment officers, called musarkisus, were in charge of the operation. Musarkisus were high-level bureaucratic officials appointed directly by the king. Each province had two horse recruitment officers and it was their job to get as many horses as they could. They would then have to train them before sending them out from the national stables for military use by both the native army and the deportees serving as auxiliary units.[7]

The reason for so many deportees was the need to protect the strategic parts of the empire. Deportees were the best solution, for the Assyrian population was far too small to cover the vast amount of conquered land. Many of the deportees had been warriors before arriving at their assigned settlement. The Assyrians would recruit the strongest and fittest men, sending them to an unknown region for training in the Assyrian martial arts and tactics.[8] For example, after the capture of Samaria by Sargon II in 721 BCE, he did not kill the warriors; he incorporated them into his army.[9] Another interesting aspect is that after training, some would stay with the Assyrian army, while others were sent back to their deported tribe to train other men. Those newly trained men would fill in the ranks of the Assyrian auxiliary units in both cavalry and infantry.[10]

The Cimmerian and Scythian peoples in the Assyrian district of Uishdish, renamed Gamir, were deportees serving under the Assyrian Empire, as mentioned.[11] Assyria would place deportees to serve, as auxiliaries to counter would be intruders that the native army could not reach. The scholar Bustenay Oded writes on the role of those deported and states:

> ... the exiled communities played a role very similar to that of the Assyrian garrisons stationed in all parts of the Assyrian empire, or to that of Assyrian citizens who were settled in conquered countries either as city dwellers, farmers, or officials. This explains the favorable treatment the deportees generally enjoyed, and the great concern shown by the Assyrian rulers for their welfare.[12]

Deportees like the Cimmerians and Scythians were settled next to other deportees who may have been a little more aggressive or hard to handle. This was designed to keep the peace through self-government, but with a watchful eye. Reflecting on this theory, if a rebellious group were to keep causing trouble, the best way to counteract it would be to bring in a new group that had been showered with the monarch's favor. Most of the rebellious deportees despised new arrivals, thinking they worked for the Assyrians to spy on them.[13] Since the new deportees received favorable treatment, they would probably be inclined to tell the Assyrian administrator of the province if there was any suspicious activity However, it worked the other way around, as well. We could say both groups watched each other, but also kept an eye on the Assyrians.

Assyrian Army Auxiliaries

As mentioned, the Assyrian military used auxiliary units to serve in the native army. Tiglath-pileser III expanded the numbers of such units. But it was Sargon II, who would make the auxiliary units common throughout the empire. Auxiliaries were "sab sharri" or levies, assembled by the provincial governor on the orders of the king. The Cimmerians likely were sab sharri, suggesting the possibility that the cavalry that rode alongside Sargon or perhaps Sin-ahi-usur at the battle on Mt. Uaush could have been Cimmerian bodyguards.[14] The total Assyrian fighting force as a whole during the Neo-Assyrian period was between 150,000 and 200,000 troops. This is not a substantial number, because no records exist on how many troops, both native and non-native, served in the Assyrian forces.

Nevertheless, the size of Assyria and the surrounding regions meant there was a great need for defense troops. The auxiliary units alone made up one-third of the total fighting force. Thus one-third of the Assyrian armed forces were not native to Assyria and were made up of those deported from their original country and settled in new lands to care for and to defend the borders and regions under Assyrian control.[15] In addition, Assyrian auxiliary troops dressed in native attire and retained their own identity. The Assyrians speak of a Cimmerian detachment known as "Kisir Gimirai" during the reign of King Esarhaddon.[16] This shows that some

Cimmerians were indeed auxiliary troops under the guidance of Assyria.

As mentioned, the first appearance of the Cimmerians is around 714 BCE, but before their appearance, Sargon II in 715 BCE had to re-conquer some fortresses taken by King Rusa of Urartu. The Cimmerians in 714 BCE populated the Mannaean border with Urartu and garrisoned the Mannae fortresses. It was normal procedure for the Assyrian administration to place foreigners from conquered territories along hostile border areas for the security of the empire. It seems plausible that Sargon had placed a conquered people in charge of a province. Therefore, the Cimmerians' role was to buffer any attacks coming in from Urartu.[17] Even though this method of placing deportees along the fringes of the Assyrian Empire was effective in border security, this also had a substantial risk for fomenting rebellion, as in the case of the Cimmerians later on.

Endnotes: Chapter One

[1] Richard A. Gabriel, *Soldiers' Lives through History - The Ancient World*, (New York: Greenwood Press, 2006), 92/ Kaveh Farrokh, *Shadows in the Desert: Ancient Persia at War* (Oxford: Osprey Publishing, 2007), 29.

[2] John W. Eadie, *The Journal of Roman* (Eadie 1967)*Studies*, Vol. 57, No. 1/2 (1967), 161-173.

[3] Gabriel, *Soldiers' Lives through History - The Ancient World*, 92.

[4] Mark Healy and Angus McBride, *The Ancient Assyrians*, (Oxford: Osprey Publishing, 2000), 9, 20, 21.

[5] Rea, 59-60, 78.

[6] V. Vuksic & Z. Grbasic, *Cavalry: The History of a Fighting Elite*, (London: Cassell, 1993), 38.

[7] Richard A. Gabriel, *The Great Armies of Antiquity*, (Westport, Conn: Praeger, 2002), 133.

[8] Serge Yalichev, *Mercenaries of the Ancient World*, (London: Constable, 1997), 72.

[9] James Maxwell Miller and John Haralson Hayes, *A History of Ancient Israel and Judah*, (Philadelphia: Westminster Press, 1986), 338.

[10] Yalichev, 72.

[11] Anne Kristensen, *Who were the Cimmerians, and where did they come from?: Sargon II, the Cimmerians, and Rusa I* (Copenhagen: Det kongelige Danske videnskabernes selskab, 1988), 92.

[12] Bustenay Oded, *Mass Deportation and Deportees in the Neo-Assyrian Empire*, (Wiesbaden: Reichert, 1979), 47.

[13] Yalichev, *Mercenaries of the Ancient World*, 72.

[14] Mark Healy and Angus McBride, *The Ancient Assyrians*, (Oxford: Osprey Publishing, 2000), 9.

[15] Richard A. Gabriel, *The Military History of Ancient Israel*, (Westport, CT: Praeger Publishers, 2003), 47.

[16] Kristensen, *Who were the Cimmerians, and where did they come from?*, 100.

[17] Ibid, 99-100.

2

Sargon's Blowback

In 714 BCE, the Assyrian crown prince Sennacherib received reports concerning troop movements of the Urartian forces. The reports were sent to King Sargon II of Assyria. It was also during this time that Sargon's eighth campaign was already in full military mode against Urartu. These reports tell us that Urartian forces invaded the land of Gamir, (formerly known as Uishdish)[1] and were defeated. The first of these reports dealing with the Gamir (Cimmerians) comes from the crown prince, Sennacherib, found in ABL 1079 (Assyrian Babylonian Letters):

> [Thi]s was the report of Aššur-reṣuwa. [Šulmu]-Bel, the deputy of the Palace Herald came into my presence (with the following report):
>
> "Urzana has written to me: 'The troops of the Urartian king have been defeated on his expedition against the Cimmerians. The governor of Waisi has been killed; we do

not have detailed information yet, but as soon as we have it, we will send you a full report."

ABL 197 states:

"To the king, my lord: your servant Sin-ahhe-riba. Good health to the king, my lord! Assyria is well, the temples are well, all the king's forts are well. The king, my lord, can be glad indeed.

The Ukkaean has sent me (this message): "The troops of the Urartian king have been utterly defeated on his expedition against the Cimmerians; eleven of his governors have been eliminated [with] their troops; his commander-in-chief and two of his governors [have been taken prisoners]. He (himself) came to take [the road to ......] came [...... the pr]efects of his country [......] stationed [in ......].

[Thi]s was the report of the Ukkaean. Aššur-reṣuwa has written to me thus:

"The previous report which I sent about the Urartians was that they had suffered a terrible defeat. Now his country is quiet again and each of his magnates has gone to his province. Kaqqadanu, his commander-in-chief, has been taken prisoner; the Urarṭian king is in the province of Wazaun."

This was the report of Aššur-reṣuwa. Nabû-le'i the governor of Birate has written to me: "I have written to the guards of the forts along the border concerning the news of the Urartian king and they (tell me this): 'His troops have been utterly defeated on his expedition against the Cimmerians. Three of his magnates along with their troops have been killed; he himself has escaped and entered his country, but his army has not yet arrived (back).'"[2]

The Urartian forces invaded Gamir and met defeat at the hands of the Cimmerians. Historian Anne Kristensen speculates whether the Cimmerians were involved in defeating the Urartians, more on this later.[3] The reports come from the vast spy network set up by Sargon, who used his border forts or cities on the border as spy centers. Each fort or city would send spies out to collect intelligence on the enemy's intentions and to keep track of the enemy's troop movements.[4] In this case, the Assyrian spies and their allies closely watched the Urartian invasion, assessing the situation and praising the outcome. This raises a few questions: was the land of Gamir part of Assyria or one of their allies, and were the Cimmerians who dwelled in the land serving under Sargon at the time?

Some historians make the mistake to conjure up the idea that an invading horde of Cimmerians crossed the Caucasus Mountains and attacked the northern frontier of the Kingdom of Urartu in 714 BCE.[5] The problem with this interpretation is there are no reports of the Cimmerians pouring down from the north through the Caucasus Mountains and into Urartu. Herodotus speaks of the Cimmerians and Scythians pouring down through the Caucasus, but this supposed event took place more than 200 years later. Hesiod in the 9th century BCE does not mention the Cimmerians or an invasion, nor does Aristeas of Proconnesus in the 7th century. In fact, no archaeological evidence indicates a large mass of people coming from the north and passing along the east coast of the Black Sea. This also applies to the area that leads through the Caucasus in the western region.[6] Conversely, the Cimmerians were dwelling in the land of Gamir, which bears their name, although the location has been in dispute for some time.

Historians, such as A.H. Sayce and A.T. Olmstead, suggest Gamir is Guriania, in Gurun, which is located in present-day Turkey. Moses of Chorene suggests Gamir is rendered as Kamir and is the name for Cappadocia.[7] Others think Gamir was northwest of Urartu in the present-day country of Georgia. Many seem not to consider that Gamir could have been to the south or southeast of Urartu. Anne Kristensen, author of *Who Were the Cimmerians, and Where Did They Come From?*, argues that the province of Gamir is located to the south or southeast of Urartu, around Lake Urmia.[8] Her reason for this location is based on ABL 112, which states:

> To the Palace Herald, my lord: your servant Urda-Sin. The Cimmerian (king) has departed from Mannea this [...] and entered Urartu. He is ... [in] Hu'diadae; Sarduri is [...] in Ṭur[u]špâ. The messenger of the governor of Wais[i] has gone to Ur[za]na for [help], saying: "Let yo[ur] troops come to (aid) the people of Pulia and Suriana." All of Urarṭu is extremely frightened. They are assembling troops, saying: "Perhaps we can attack him, once there is more snow." As to this booty which they said he has taken, they do say that of the district of Arhi, [...]......[9]

Notice the inscription mentions the Cimmerians "went forth from the midst of the Mannai and into the land of Urartu." Now, when you read ABL 112 and compare it to ABL 197 the support for Gamir being south and east of Lake Urmia seems plausible. In other words, ABL 197 illustrates that the King of Urartu invaded the lands of Gamir and was defeated by the Cimmerians. Afterwards, the Cimmerian forces left the province of Gamir, which is a part of Mannea, and invaded the lands of Urartu.[10]

There are two reasons Gamir/Uishdish is important. The forts: King Rusa understood that Uishdish is of strategic significance due to the forts dotting the landscape. The second reason concerns the sphere of influence over Mannea. In 716 BCE, Rusa influenced two Mannean governors, Bagdatti of Uishdish and Metatti of Zikirtu, to rebel against Sargon. They would succeed in killing King Aza of Mannea. Sargon's forces would capture Bagdatti, charging him with the murder of Aza, promoting rebellion, and conspiring with the enemy. Afterwards, the Assyrians took him to Mt. Uaush and flayed him alive. Had King Rusa succeeded, Mannea would have been an Urartian vassal state acting as a buffer zone between them and Assyria. Assyria, of course, wanted to keep it the other way around.[11]

Even though Sargon had retaken the fortresses from Rusa, giving them over to King Ullusunu of Mannea, Aza's brother, Rusa, returned around 715 BCE and captured 22 fortresses. The provincial Mannaean governor responsible for allowing Rusa to take the fortresses was Daiaukku. Both Daiaukku and Rusa conspired against both Mannae and Assyria. However, once the fog cleared, the Assyrians would capture and deport Daiaukku, and Sargon would go on to recapture the 22 fortresses. However, Sargon then would incorporate them into the Assyrian territory. King Ullusunu would hold temporary ownership over the fortresses; meantime, Sargon placed Assyrian and Mannae troops throughout the forts of Uishdish. However, Rusa invaded Uishdish again and possibly assumed control of all the forts,[12] but the region seems to have remained in Cimmerian hands according to ABL 112.[13] When Rusa captured the territory of Uishdish in 714 BCE, Sargon was conducting military operations in Zikirtu. Thus, ABL 112 suggests that the Cimmerians were living in the land named after them, which also suggests that the Cimmerians were the troops who garrisoned the forts at Uishdish/Gamir when Rusa arrived. With this said, we can now turn to "The Letter to Assur."

"The Letter to Assur," by Sargon, is an account of his victory over the forces of Urartu on Mt. Uaush. The account of Sargon's victory is a vivid detailed picture of the events that transpired before and during the battle. We shall focus on the parts of the letters that are relevant to the question and connection. Assur Letters 154-155 have a connection with both ABL 197 and ABL 112. Assur Letter 154 states:

> I was not afraid of his masses of troops, I despised his horses, I did not cast a glance at the multitude of his mail-clad(?) warriors. With my single chariot and the horse(men) who go at my side, who never leave (me) either in a hostile or friendly region, the troop, the command of Sin-ahi-usur, I plunged into the midst like a swift (lit., frightful) javelin, I defeated him, I turned back his advance; I killed large numbers of his (troops), the bodies of his warriors I cut down like millet(?), filling the mountain valleys (with them).

Assur Letter 155 states: "I defeated the armies of Urartu, the wicked enemy, and their allies, in the midst of Uaush Mountain he came to a stop."[14]

Both letters tell us that Sargon along with Sin-ahi-usur defeated the Urartian forces at Mt. Uaush located in Uishdish/Gamir. When reading ABL 197 and ABL 112 and comparing it with Assur letters 154-155, we get a picture of two battles taking place around the same time, but in fact, there is only one battle, the same battle, to which both letters refer. Here is the difference. The Assur letter is the overall battle itself, written as an epic poem of victory that sums up both ABL 197 and ABL 112. ABL 197 is the beginning of the battle on Mt. Uaush and its aftermath. ABL 112, like ABL 197, details the follow-up after the victory. In other words, King Rusa invaded and was defeated by the Cimmerians in the land of Gamir, which was under Cimmerian control, and this suggests the Cimmerians were a part of the Assyrian fighting force. After the victory, the Cimmerians made a counterattack, leaving the province of Mannae and invading the Kingdom of Urartu.

Now, it is possible that when Rusa invaded the lands of Gamir, he first engaged the forts garrisoned by Assyrian, Cimmerian, and Mannaean forces, before the initial battle took place. Rusa may have taken a few forts or all of them. Sargon gets word of the event and moves towards Gamir, and victory soon follows. But there is another question: was or was not Sargon at the battle on

Mt. Uaush? This is a boggling question because in the Assur Letter, Sargon states:

> With my single chariot and the horse(men) who go at my side, who never leave (me) either in a hostile or friendly region, the troop, the command of Sin-ahi-usur, I plunged into the midst like a swift (lit., frightful) javelin.[15]

The statement is quite odd. Sargon makes this very bold statement and then mentions a commander by the name of Sin-ahi-usur with him at the battle. Anne Kristensen points out that in the annals of Assyrian history, few commanders are mentioned alongside the king in battle. Kristensen also points to another inscription concerning Sargon at Ashdod. The Ashdod inscriptions is somewhat similar to the Assur letter and reads, "In the anger of my heart, with my own chariot and with my cavalry, who in a hostile land never leave my side, to Ashdod, his royal city, quickly I marched."[16]

After reading the various inscriptions and comparing them with Assur Letter 154, we begin to see a similarity, leading to the question of whether Sargon physically was at the battle on Mt. Uaush. Both ABL 1097 and ABL 197 mention the defeat of the Urartian forces in the land of Gamir. Notice the letters are addressed to Sargon. Even though they do not mention him by name, they are reports Sargon would have read, updating him on the current situation. This suggests Sargon was not at the battle, but somewhere else. Nevertheless, Sargon may have been at the battle on Mt. Uaush along with Sin-ah-usur. However, according to the statements made in ABL 1097, ABL 197, ABL 112, and the Assur Letter, only one out of four mentions Sargon being at the battle. Therefore, Sargon's presence at the battle is possible, but highly doubtful. Instead, Sin-ah-usur led not Assyrian forces, but rather Cimmerian cavalry forces fighting under the banner of Assyria that ultimately defeated King Rusa and his forces.[17]

Cimmerian Rebellion

With the Urartu-Assyria war resulting in an Assyrian victory, Sargon could rest assured that his borders to the north were safe for the time being. Sargon had other problems to deal with, such as Babylonia, which had a history of rebellion. Thus in 710 BCE, Sargon went down to Babylonia, and in a two-year struggle, he was able to reassert Assyrian authority around 708/07 BCE. The victory over Babylonia caused many to bow down to Sargon, sending him gifts as a gesture of peace and capitulation, including Dilmun (Bahrain), Iatnana (Cyprus), and Midas, king of Phrygia. Midas offered his friendship as a gift to Sargon.[18]

The king's word to Aššur-šarru-u[ṣur]: I am well, Assyria is well: you can be glad.

As to what you wrote to me: "A messenger [of] Midas the Phrygian has come to me, bringing me 14 men of Que whom Urik had sent to Urarṭu as an embassy" — this is extremely good! My gods Aššur, Šamaš, Bel and Nabû have now taken action, and without a battle [or any]thing, the Phrygian has given us his word and become our ally![19]

Before Midas made his peace offering to Sargon, he was a supporter of Urartu during the Urartu-Assyrian war in 714 BCE. When Urartu lost the war, Sargon continued his conquest towards the west, pursuing those who were Urartu supporters, such as King Ambaris of Tabal. Ambaris submitted to Sargon's yoke by marrying his daughter, princess Akhat-abisha, forming not only a royal family bond, but also making Tabal a vassal to Assyria. However, in 713 BCE, he was arrested for plotting against Sargon by allying himself with Urartu and Phrygia; thus Ambaris' wife, Akhat-abisha, may have ruled Tabal after Sargon annexed Tabal in 713 BCE;[20] more on Tabal shortly.

Now, why would King Midas offer peace to Sargon? It is possible Assyria was conducting raids in Phrygia before King Midas asked for peace. Remember, King Midas asked for peace between him and Sargon. One of the reasons Midas asked for peace was fear of a possible

Cimmerian invasion of his kingdom.[21] The possibility of Cimmerian auxiliaries loyal to Assyria conducting raids into Phrygia is not farfetched. Sargon might have threatened Midas with attack if he did not comply with Assyria's power. Or we can deduce that the presence of Cimmerians in some form of action, whether directly or indirectly, caused Midas to reach out for peaceful measures. We shall discuss more on King Midas a little later, but for now, let us focus on the province of Tabal.

Before Midas made peace with Assyria, Sargon subjugated Tabal in 713 BCE.[22] Why is this of importance, one may ask? The importance of the issue is the possibility that the Cimmerians conducted raids on Phrygia from Tabal. There is no proof of this, for there is no letter, no inscription, no nothing, but the possibility exists. After the subjugation of Tabal by Assyria and Phrygia requesting peace, a rebellion arose in Tabal. No one is certain as to what caused the rebellion. However, it is obvious those in Tabal revolted because they were not interested in Assyrian subjugation, and the Cimmerian detachment stationed there may have felt the same way.

In 705 BCE, a Cimmerian chieftain by the name of Eshpai led rebellion revolt against Assyria. Sargon was not going to put up with this insurrection, which could lead to the destabilization of his empire. When Sargon arrived with his forces, an unforeseen death awaited him. Unfortunately there is nothing known about how the battle looked or how they squared off against one another.

The battle was so violent and so chaotic and the Cimmerians were powerful enough to push right through the remaining Assyrian ranks and through the royal guards to reach Sargon and kill him. The Assyrian inscriptions mention little of this event and are quite vague about every detail other than Sargon's death.

> The king [against Tabal ....] against Ešpai the Kulummaean. [......] The king was killed. The camp of the king of Assyria [was taken ......]. On the 12th of Abu, Sennacherib, son [of Sargon, took his seat on the throne].[23]

The inscription regarding Kulummaean may be correct, but on the original mutilated tablet, the letters *Gi* are visible. Following this, the next visible letter is *m*. If so, the word Gi-mir-a-a-a was once visible on the tablet.[24] On the inscription, the name Espai is disputed and is suggested to be read as "Gurdi." In addition, the battle may have not taken place in Tabal, but rather in Western Iran, in the Harhar province.[25] The reason is that the name Kulummaean may be the name of a city located in Harhar, known as Kuluman or Kilman.[26] The difficulty is determining where the battle took place. If we support the idea that the battle took place in the province of Tabal, we may have to consider that Espai or Gurdi is a Cimmerian from the city of Kuluman or Kilman, who happened to lead not only the native troops in Tabal, but also the Cimmerian auxiliaries stationed in the region. The second possibility is that Espai or Gurdi is from the city Kuluman or Kilman and led an army primarily made up of Cimmerians along with other forces based in the Harhar province, where the actual battle took place and where Sargon died. I do not rule out either conjecture.

After Sargon's death in battle, his personal camp is captured by the Cimmerians. His body was taken back to be buried with honors by his son, Sennacherib.[27] Even this is vague, as Sennacherib does not go into much detail about the campaign or his father's death, nor does Sennacherib return to the area of battle for revenge during his reign. The tablet discussing Sargon's death seems to indicate something much worse happened. It is quite possible that the Cimmerians took the body of Sargon.[28] With his death, the idea of a full-scale rebellion was born. The once seemingly invincible Assyrian king was now dead. After the death of Sargon, the Cimmerians seem to have disappeared. Some 35 years would pass before they reappeared in Assyrian inscriptions. No text mentions them by name during the reign of Sennacherib, but they often were mentioned during the reign of Sennacherib's son, Esarhaddon.[29] Because of this, we should not think the Cimmerians and Assyrians broke off contact with one another. They most definitely were, for there was a Cimmerian detachment that served under King Esarhaddon. The Cimmerians and Assyrians were, for the most part, working together, while other Cimmerian elements seem to have gone with Assyria's enemies or were working for personal gain.

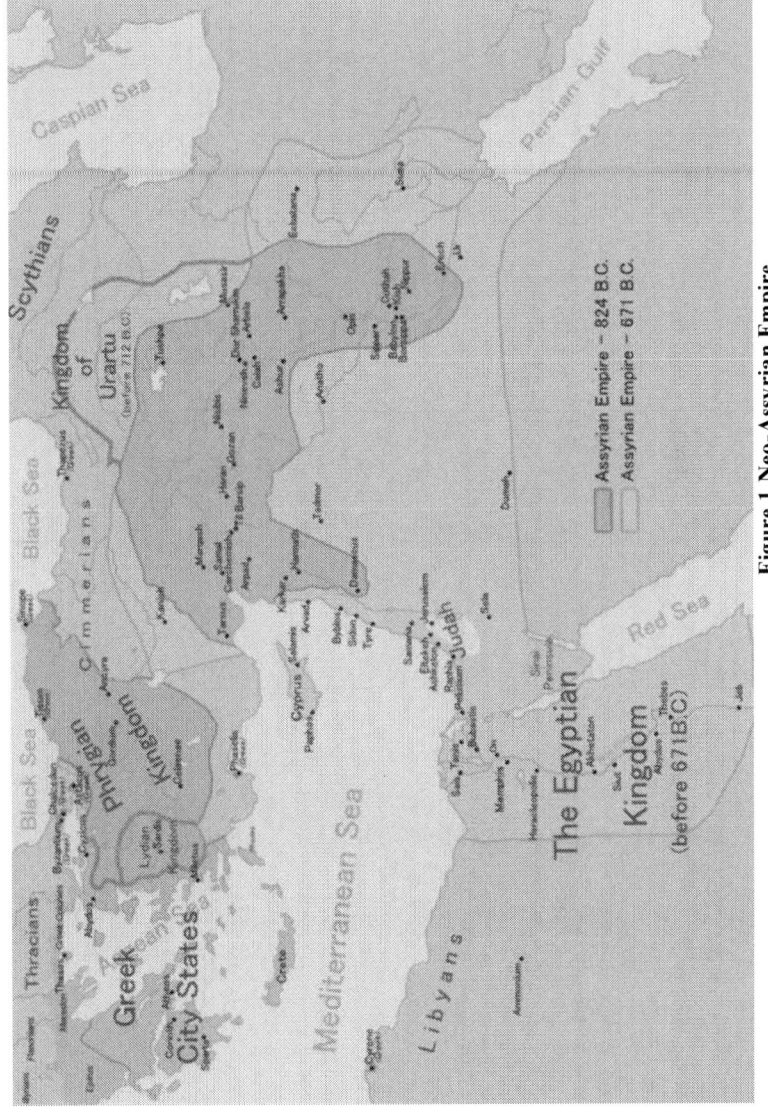

Figure 1 Neo-Assyrian Empire

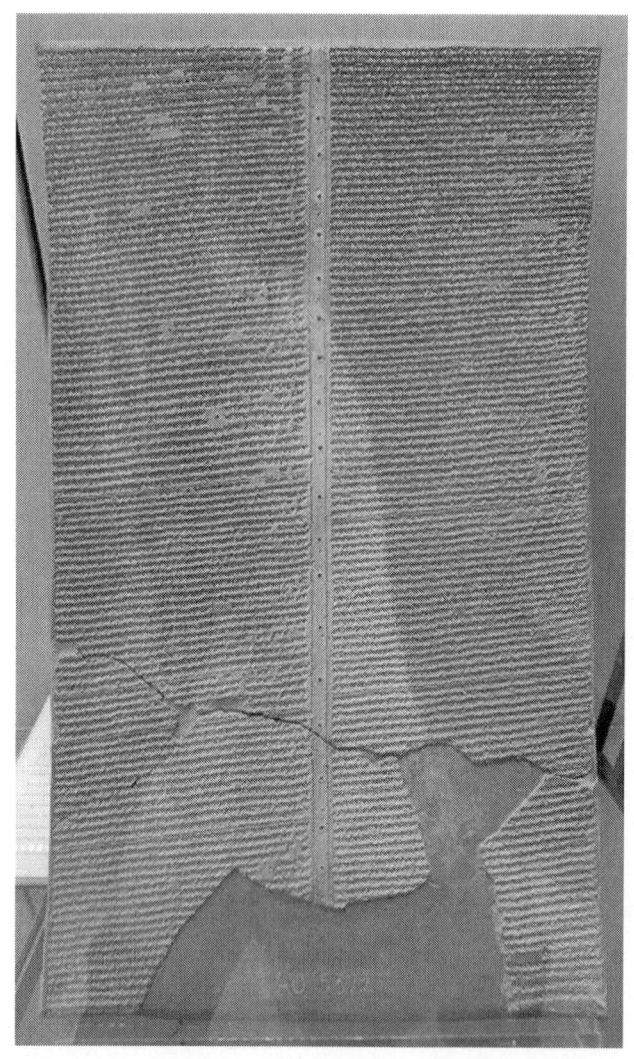

Figure 2 History of the eighth campaign of Sargon II, king of Assyria, against Urartu. 714 BC, found in Assur[31]

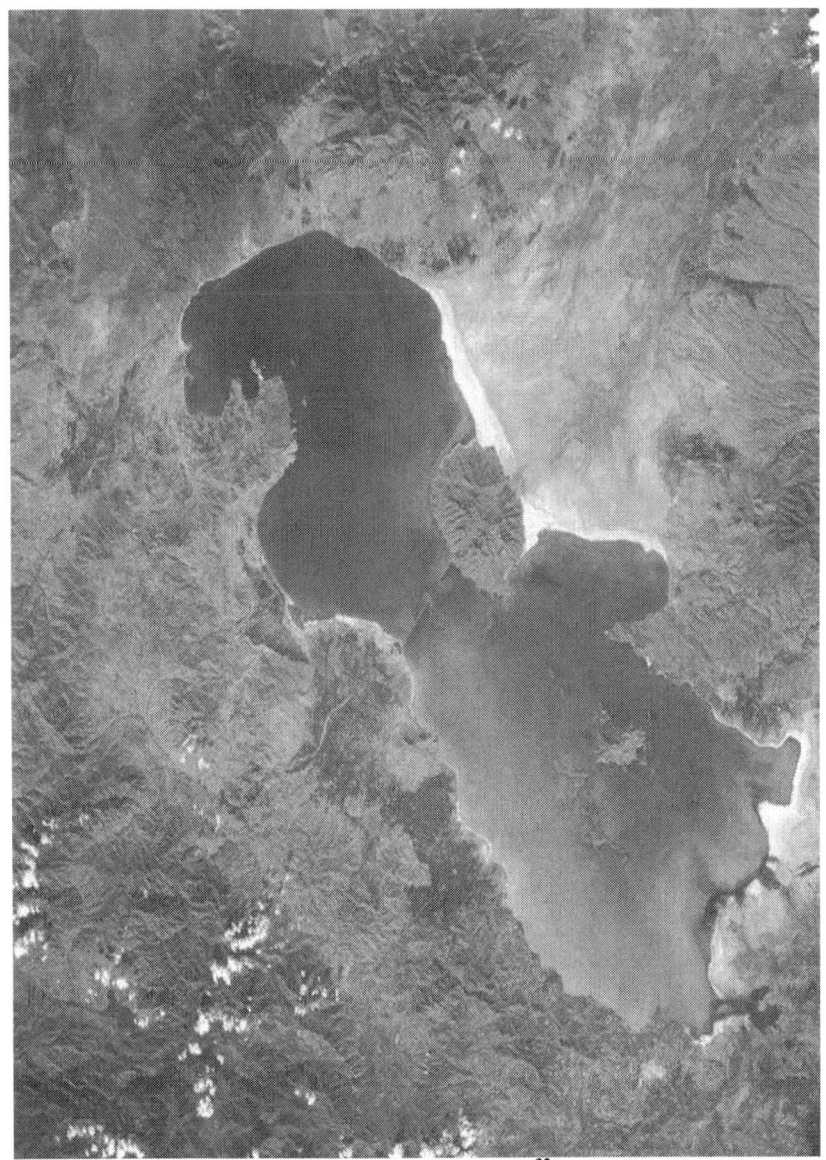

Figure 3 Lake Urmia[32]

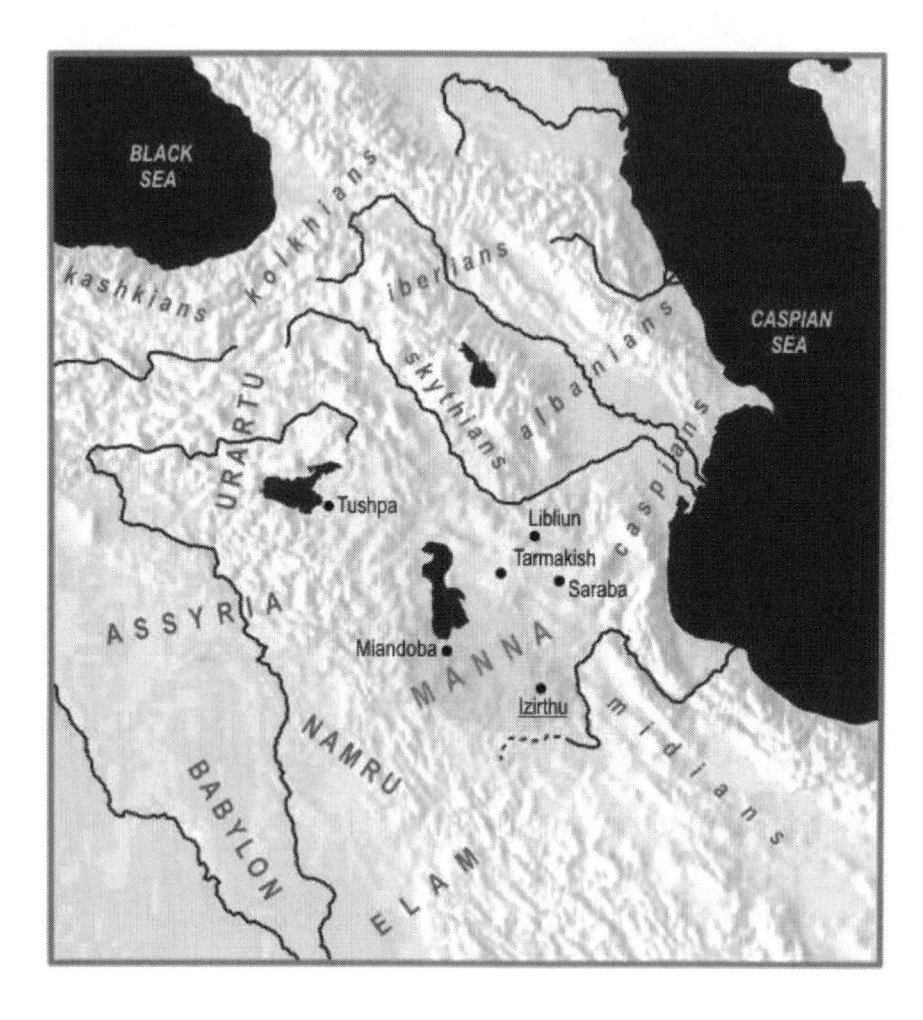

Figure 4 Manna[33]

Endnotes: Chapter Two

[1] Kristensen, 92.
[2] Simo Parpola, *The Correspondence of Sargon II, Part I: Letters from Assyria and the West State Archives of Assyria, Volume I,* (Helsinki: Helsinki University Press, 1987), 30-31.
[3] Kristensen, 88.
[4] Harry A. Hoffner, Gary A. Beckman, *Letters from the Hittite Kingdom,* (Atlanta, GA: Society of Biblical Literature, 2009), 23.
[5] M. Chahin, *The Kingdom of Armenia*, (New York:Dorset Press, 1991), 86.
[6] Ilya Gershevitch, *The Cambridge History of Iran, Volume 2: The Median and Achaememian Periods*, (Cambridge: Cambridge University Press, 1985), 93.
[7] A. H. Sayce, *The Kingdom of Van (Urartu),* (CAH III: Cambridge, 1965), 182. & A. H. Sayce, *Decipherment of Hittite Inscriptions*, (PSBA 25, London, 1903) 148. A. T. Olmstead, *Western Asia in the Days of Sargon of Assyria,* (New York, 1908), 92. & A. T. Olmstead, *History of Assyria*, (Chicago and London, reprint, 1975. (1923), 155 note 35, 266.
[8] Kristensen, 18-20.
[9] Giovanni B. Lanfranchi and Simo Parpola, *The Correspondence of Sargon II, Part II: Letters from the Northern and Northeastern Provinces State Archives of Assyria, Volume V*, (Helsinki: Helsinki University Press, 1990), 145.
[10] Parpola, *The Correspondence of Sargon II, Part I: Letters from Assyria and the West State Archives of Assyria, Volume I,* 30-31.
[11] Kristensen, 48-49
[12] Ibid, 49-54.
[13] Lanfranchi and Parpola, *The Correspondence of Sargon II, Part II: Letters from the Northern and Northeastern Provinces State Archives of Assyria, Volume V*, 145.
[14] Daniel David Luckenbill, *Ancient Records of Assyria and Babylonia. Volume I: Historical Records of Assyria, from the earliest times to Sargon. Volume II: Historical Records of Assyria, from Sargon to the end.* (Chicago: University Of Chicago Press, 1926.), 81-83.
[15] . Luckenbill, *Ancient Records of Assyria and Babylonia. Volume I: Historical Records of Assyria, from the earliest times to Sargon. Volume II*, 82.
[16] Kristensen, 86-87.
[17] Ibid, 86-98.
[18] George Roux, *Ancient Iraq*, (Boston: Penguin, 1993), 314.

[19] Parpola, *The Correspondence of Sargon II, Part I: Letters from Assyria and the West State Archives of Assyria, Volume I*, 1.
[20] Gwendolyn Leick, *Who's who in the Ancient Near East*, (New York: Routledge, 1999), 8, 12-13.
[21] Muhammad A. Dandamaev, Vladimir G. Lukonin, Philip L. Kohl, D. J. Dadson, *The Culture and Social Institutions of Ancient Iran*, (New York: Cambridge University Press, 2004), 51.
[22] Leick, *Who's who in the Ancient Near East*, 12-13.
[23] H. Tadmor, *Journal of Cuneiform Studies, vol. XII, no. 3: The Campaigns of Sargon II of Assur; Chronology. Eine Eriderung*, (New York: American Schools Of Oriental Research, 1958), 85.
[24] Robert Drews, *Early Riders: The Beginnings of Mounted Warfare in Asia and Europe*, (New York" Routledge, 2004), 96.
[25] John David Hawkins, *Corpus of Hieroglyphic Luwian Inscriptions: Inscriptions of the Iron Age (Untersuchungen Zur Indogermanischen Sprach- Und Kulturwissenschaft, N.F., 8.1) (Three Volume Set)*, (Berlin: Walter De Gruyter, 2000), 428. Note 50.
[26] Gershevitch, *The Cambridge History of Iran (Volume 2)*, 87. Note 1.
[27] Robert Rogers, *A History of Babylonia & Assyria*, (New York: The Abingdon Press, 1915), 347.
[28] Steven Holloway, *Assur Is King! Assur Is King!*, (Leiden: Brill Academic Publishers, 2002), 138.
[29] Askold I. Ivantchik, *Les Cimmerians au Proche-Orient*, (Switzerland: Vandenhoeck & Ruprecht, 1993), 57.
[30] Ningyou, Map of the Assyrian Empire," Photograph. *http://en.wikipedia.org/* http://en.wikipedia.org/wiki/File:Map_of_Assyria.png. 26 February 2006. Web, 5 Sept. 2012.
[31] "Terracotta tablet relating the 8th campaign of Sargon II, king of Assyria, against Urartu. 714 BC, found in Assur." Photograph. *http://commons.wikimedia.org* http://commons.wikimedia.org/wiki/File:8th_campaign_Sargon_Louvre_AO5372.jpg. 14 June 2006. Department of Oriental Antiquities, Richelieu, ground floor, room 6. Web, 4 Sept. 2012.
[32] NASA, "Lake Urmia, Iran," Photograph. *http://commons.wikimedia.org* http://en.wikipedia.org/wiki/File:Lake_urmia.jpg. Web, 4 Sept. 2012.
[33] "Manna," Photograph. *http://az.wikipedia.org/* http://az.wikipedia.org/wiki/%C5%9E%C9%99kil:Manna_ilkin_yaranma_v%C9%99_geni%C5%9Fl%C9%99nm%C9%99.jpg. 11 August 2009. Web, 5 Sept. 2012.

3

Esarhaddon's Curse

During the reign of King Sennacherib, the Assyrians had no issues of conflict with the Cimmerians, for all was quiet. Further west, an old friend was having a moment with them. The old friend in question is King Midas of Phrygia, who sued for peace, as mentioned in the Assyrian inscriptions during the reign of Sargon II. The reason he sued for peace is unclear, but it could have been that he feared a Cimmerian threat sponsored by Assyria. Nevertheless, the next question is: did the Cimmerians destroy Phrygia, causing Midas to commit suicide?

Midas appears in the Assyrian inscriptions as "Mita of Muski."[1] The details of a Cimmerian invasion that destroyed his kingdom are vague. Many ancient historians mentioned Midas, but the details concerning a Cimmerian invasion are almost non-existent. The historian Strabo mentions Midas' suicide by drinking bull's blood, but is the first to mention it in connection with the Cimmerian invasion.

> And those Cimmerians whom they also call Trerans (or some tribe or other of the Cimmerians) often overran the countries on

> the right of the Pontus and those adjacent to them, at one time having invaded Paphlagonia, and at another time Phrygia even, at which time Midas drank bull's blood, they say, and thus went to his doom.[2]

Plutarch also mentions Midas' death due to drinking bull's blood. He does not mention an invading horde as the precipitate cause of his death, but rather dreams that caused him to commit suicide.

> Midas of old, dispirited and disturbed, as it appears, as the result of some dreams, reached such a state of mind that he committed suicide by drinking bull's blood.[3]

The drinking of bull's blood was a trial by ordeal.[4] Midas wanted to know if the gods favored him or not. Nevertheless, bull's blood is not potent enough to kill a person. The bull's blood Midas drank most likely was either putrefied or poisoned.[5] To say Midas committed suicide may be inaccurate, since he was weighing the will of the gods to see whom they found favorable. In this case, the Cimmerians are the favored. This leaves us with a question; did the Cimmerians invade and destroy his capital?

The Cimmerian invasion is said to have taken place roughly around 696/695 BCE, according to the *Chronicle of Jerome*[6] and Eusebius.[7] Archeologists remain divided over the issue due to the limited destruction found. Moreover, no artifacts discovered at Gordion can be associated with the Cimmerians. However, the name "MM" discovered at Gordion is most likely associated with King Midas. In addition, test results from Gordion suggest Cimmerians are not the ones who destroyed it. The test results indicate the supposed damage was from around the second half of the 9th century BCE, thus disqualifying the Cimmerians as the cause.[8]

The results seem obvious in the Midas investigation. There was no Cimmerian invasion of Gordion in 696/695 BCE. Had an invasion occurred, the Assyrians would most likely have mentioned it. This, however, does not mean an invasion by the Cimmerians did not take place, but we must wait until further evidence is uncovered. For now, we do know there was a King Midas, but how long he lived after Sargon's death remains unknown, as well as his relationship to Sennacherib.

Esarhaddon's Northern Trouble

Esarhaddon ascended the throne in 680 BCE due to violence. His father, King Sennacherib, was murdered by Esarhaddon's older brother, Arda-Mulissu. The murder of the king sent Assyria into civil unrest and rebellion sprang forth throughout the empire.[9]

King Esarhaddon's first order of business was to salvage the trust of Assyria's old allies and put down the ongoing rebellions. More importantly, Esarhaddon would "extend his hand" to those living in Media in order to regain their trust. Esarhaddon wanted the various nomads as allies for another purpose. His motive was to gain support for his choice of who would sit upon the thrones of Assyria and Babylonia when he died. The idea was to prevent another civil war or mass rebellion. Why did Esarhaddon trust the people in and around Media? The answer could be that he actually feared them. It is possible that vast numbers of Cimmerians and Scythians, as well as other nomadic tribes, were living in Media on peaceful terms with Assyria. Assyria, in turn, acknowledged the strength of the Cimmerians, Scythians, and Medes as being a potential if not equal threat. It seems the various tribes living within Media pretended to be interested, but as time went on, the Assyrian belief that those living in Media would support and protect their interests would vanish.[10]

In 680 BCE, a new king by the name of Rusa II ascended the throne of Urartu.[11] Rusa II was no friend of Assyria, no surprise. He appears to be enough of a threat to cause Esarhaddon to worry. The reason Esarhaddon worried is clear, but the chronology of the events are not. Nevertheless, we are not at a complete loss. Therefore, let us look back briefly to Esarhaddon's concerns.

As previously mentioned, Esarhaddon's older brother Arda-Mulissu murdered their father Sennacherib with the help of an accomplice. According to the Bible in the book of (II Kings 19:37) it states:

> And it came to pass, as he was worshiping in the house of Nisroch his god, that Adrammelech and Sharezer his sons smote him with the sword: and they escaped into the land of Armenia. And his son reigned in his stead.[12]

The two names mentioned, Adrammelech and Sharezer are in question, but more important than the names itself is the fact that they fled to Armenia. The name Armenia really corresponds to Urartu. The reason both men fled to the Kingdom of Urartu is obvious: it was a safe haven. From Urartu, the guilty can collude with the enemies of Assyria, particularly Rusa II. Esarhaddon understood that his brother, brothers, or anyone involved, would make a challenge for the Assyrian throne from Urartu if the opportunity presented itself. However, Urartu would need a strong army to complete such an endeavor. This could be the reason why Rusa II and his father Argishti II reached out to the Cimmerians and Scythians.

Argishti II rebuilt the Kingdom of Urartu after Sargon's death. There is no record of events recorded in Assyrian annuls that speak of Urartu during Sennacherib's reign. This is likely due to the various wars preoccupying Sennacherib. However, according to Urartu inscriptions, Argishti was busy building up his border towns and forts, whether building them anew or re-strengthening them as before Sargon II's campaign into the region. In doing so, Argishti would encounter the Cimmerian and Scythian peoples living on the fringes of the Assyrian Empire and most likely established a friendship with them. Rusa continued that friendship established by his father for political and military reasons. The proof is scattered at the fortress of Teishebaini, where archeologists have discovered weapons and ornaments connected to the Cimmerian and Scythians. Teishebaini was the Urartu military center in Transcaucasia.[13]

This may be the reason Esarhaddon wanted the loyalty of the various nomadic tribes in and around Media who served Assyria faithfully under his grandfather Sargon II. It is also possible that some served faithfully under his father, Sennacherib. This may indicate either Assyria was weak militarily and could not afford a new theater of war, or demonstrates that the various Cimmerian and Scythian tribes were strong–strong enough to challenge the might of Assyria. Both may be correct, for Esarhaddon questions and fears the intentions of Rusa II and those who follow as in the case of Teushpa.

Teushpa

Tesupha was the first of many nomadic chieftains to harass King Esarhaddon of Assyria. Unfortunately, information about Tesupha, other than what Esarhaddon provides, is scant. The event, dated sometime around 679 BCE[14] according to the inscriptions of Esarhaddon, tell us that Tesupha was king of the Cimmerians or Umman-manda, sometimes rendered as Zab Manda. They were all one and the same. We shall discuss the Umman-manda later. Esarhaddon describes Tesupha in three different inscriptions, which are roughly the same:

> Teushpa of Gimirrai, the Umman-manda whose home is remote, in the land of Hubushna, besides the whole of his army, I destroyed with the sword; (and) I trampled upon the necks of the men of the country Cilicia, and the country of Duha, the inhabitants of the forest (or hills) which are opposite the country of Tabal who upon the strength of their (strong) mountains had trusted and from the days of old did not submit to my yoke, twenty-one of their strong cities, together with the small cities which bordered them I besieged, I captured, I spoiled (them) of their spoil; I threw down, I dug up, with fire I burned. The remainder of them, who rebellion and curses had not (uttered), the heavy yoke of my lordship I placed (stood) upon them.[15]

> Teuspa, a Gimirrai, a soldier fugitive, whose place was far off in the land of Khubusna, with all his followers I brought into servitude.[16]

> Teuspa, the Cimmerian, an exiled warrior, whose place was afar in the land of

Hubusqa, with all his soldiers, I pierced with arrows.[17]

The inscriptions inform that Teushpa is from Gimirrai and is a Gimirrai (i.e., Cimmerian whose home was far away in a place called Hubushna or Khubusna, which is said to be located northwest of Assyria in a region of Cilicia, which is now a part of modern day Turkey, located to the southeast, bordering Syria. The rest of the first inscription details Esarhaddon's conquest of the region after the battle with the Teushpa. What we can gather concerning his battle against Teushpa is that Teushpa is a Cimmerian, an exiled Cimmerian at that, who was from the land of Cimmeria, which is Gimirrai or Gamir in Sargon's inscriptions. Not only is he a Cimmerian, he is a "fugitive." Esarhaddon makes it clear that Teushpa is a deserter, someone who flees from justice, particularly Assyrian justice. This would suggest that Teushpa was once an Assyrian auxiliary soldier living in the province of Gamirrai/Gamir along with his detachment In addition, the inscriptions suggest that Assyria won the battle, but the victory is not as great as Esarhaddon portrayed it.

Askold I. Ivantchik suggests that the inscription is an "exaggeration" by Esarhaddon due to the tone of the text.[18] I agree, for the inscription sounds more like a rambling of what Esarhaddon wanted to do as opposed to what he actually had done.

Nevertheless, Esarhaddon had won the day, but most likely lost more than he wanted to. The next two inscriptions are a rehash of the battle telling us what we already know, that the Cimmerians were defeated, but with a twist. One account says they are "brought into servitude," while the other says they are "pierced with arrows." Both accounts agree with one another. Esarhaddon had won the battle, but the inscriptions indicate the turnout to be far more disastrous, a victory fraught with defeat, a "Pyrrhic victory." In addition, there is another question to consider concerning Teushpa. The inscriptions mentioning Teushpa never reveal whether Assyria killed or captured him. Instead, the inscriptions mention his army as being defeated. Teushpa may have returned to Gamir, for Gamir is close to Urartu, which would provide a safety net due to the possible alliance. Therefore, Teushpa probably sought asylum in Urartu--or maybe he just disappeared. Teushpa's whereabouts after the battle will remain unknown. The threat to Assyria's northern borders was far from over, for where Tesuhpa failed, Ishpaka would try.

Ishpaka

After defeating the Cimmerians led by Teushpa in 679 BCE, a new nomadic leader arose from the northern frontier, and his name is Ishpaka.[19] Once again, little is mentioned about Ishpaka other than the fact that he is a Scythian and led a campaign along with the Manneans against Assyria. Because of this, Esarhaddon shows worry over the issue in his prayers to the Sun-god Samas.

will the troops of the S[cyth]ia[ns, which have been staying in the district of Mannea and which are (now) moving out from the territory] of Mannea, strive and plan?[20]

Esarhaddon is troubled; imminent danger from the north rears its head again. The Scythians rally under the banner of Ishpaka, who made an alliance with those living within the province of Mannea, and may have been on friendly terms with the Kingdom of Urartu. This caused enormous concern. Esarhaddon, once again, was faced with another hostile uprising being coordinated by the same people. Unlike the last location of engagement, this was much closer and had the potential to spill over into Assyria's own backyard through the Hubuskian passes.

Esarhaddon understood that the defense of the passes was crucial, for the Hubuskian passes run through the Zagros Mountains and into Northern Assyria. Once through the passes, the Scythians would be only about 100 miles northeast of Nineveh.[21] Esarhaddon realized that if the Hubuskian passes were not dammed up with Assyrian troops, a flood of Scythians, Mannaeans, and possibly Urartian forces, would go unchecked, leaving a portion of Northern Assyria open for conquest by the invaders if not countered soon. Esarhaddon gave the order to send troops not only to secure the passes, but to go into the provinces occupied by the Scythians and Mannaeans and rout them.

> "Enter into the midst of the Mannai," all the troops should not enter. Let the cavalry and the Dakku invade the Gimiraa (Cimmerians), who have spoken saying, "The Mannai pertain to you, we have not interfered." Certainly this is a lie.

Esarhaddon did not hesitate and knew he could not afford another debacle like the one with Tesupha in 679 BCE, where losses equaled that of the defeated enemy. The inscription indicates that Esarhaddon split his forces in two. One went into the province of Mannea, while the other invaded Gimirra. What is fascinating about the inscription is how Esarhaddon deals with the threat. He sends his cavalry forces into Gimirra along with the Dakku. The Assyrians understood that infantry alone would not defeat the Scythians; thus the need for cavalry to match the enemy:

> They are the offspring of outcasts, they recognize neither the oath of a god nor a (human) agreement. Let the chariots and baggage wagons take up a position on either side of the pass; (then) with the horses and the Dakku, let them enter and take the plunder of the plain of the Mannai; and let them return and at the pass let them bivouac...... once or twice they shall enter and...... plunder and the Gimiraa

(Cimmerians)..... they come, the troops......shall enter against the cities of the Mannai...... Belhabu of the Mannai..... they will change to the hands of the king my lord....... on the fifteenth day the moon appears with the sun. This is against them. Will you restrain the feet of the Cimmerians from them? If they approach, their coming and going of any sort I know not? I have sent a message to the king my lord. May the lord of kings inquire of a man acquainted with the country and may the king, at his pleasure, send to his troops raiders in addition to the (other) fighting men. A fortress there against the enemy do you provision for yourself. Let all the troops enter the Gududanu.[22]

Again, another inscription same message, with the same objective, and that is to plunder, raid, and pillage the land of the Mannea and Gimirra. Another thing to notice in the inscription is the hit, raid, and run attacks are to last for a number of days, with the Assyrian forces bivouacking outside the Hubuskian passes. The Assyrians would eventually gain the upper hand over Mannea and come to an agreement with the Scythians, but the overall result was indeed an Assyrian victory that brought Mannea back into the sphere of Assyrian influence. The inscription also suggests the battle tactics used by the Assyrians was more or less guerrilla warfare. They had to hit and run a number of times to make the enemy capitulate. This type of tactic conducted by the Assyrians may be a sign that they were unable to take the Mannean and Scythian forces head on, but rather had to pick them apart and demoralize them, in order to set up a conventional battle and ensure victory. Whatever the case may be, the inscription suggests that Esarhaddon won another costly victory. However, Esarhaddon has this to say about the outcome:

> I scattered the men of the country of Van (Mannai), Gutium disobedient, who the armies of Ispaka (king of the country of the (Asguzai) Scythians, a rebel force, not saving him (I) had overwhelmed with weapons.[23]

Even though Esarhaddon had overcome Ishpaka and his forces, it was not the end. Another Scythian leader would rise up, but this Scythian chieftain extended his hand offering peace, and his name was Bartatua.

Bartatua

Bartatua, whom Herodotus refers to as Protothyes,[24] was a Scythian chieftain or king whose reign began around 678 BCE and lasted until about 645 BCE. Bartatua is yet another shadowy figure where information is lacking. Some historians suggest Bartatua was the son of the recently defeated Ishpaka and thus his successor.[25] No one is certain, but the plausibility of Bartatua being connected to Ishpaka seems as certain as not. Nevertheless, we are not entirely at a loss, for even though his relations to other Scythian chieftains are in question, the region he resides in is not. One has to speculate on whether or not Bartatua might have resided in the city of Sakiz.

The city or village of Sakiz is located south of Lake Urmia. Sakiz was the presumed capital of the Scythians, but since the Assyrian inscriptions seem silent concerning a place named Sakiz, the importance of the city seems to be non-existent, at least in Assyrian sources. This is not to say the place did not exist, rather that the Assyrians may have been skeptical of its importance when considering the region the Scythians controlled under Bartatua as a whole.[26]

Bartatua knew what was best for his people. If they were to continue to dwell north of Assyria, then it was time to settle the hostilities. On the other hand, Esarhaddon also understood it was in Assyria's best interest to secure peace in the north. How Esarhaddon was going to do this is unknown; however, Bartatua, king of the Scythians, sent a message to Esarhaddon:

> Šamaš, great lord, give me a firm positive answer to what I am asking you!
> Bartatua, king of the Scythians, who has now sent his messengers to

> Esarhaddon, king of Assyria, concerning a royal daughter in marriage —
>
> if Esarhaddon, king of [Assyria], gives him a royal daughter in marriage, will Bartatua, king of the Scythians, speak with [Esarhaddon, king of Assyria], in good faith, true and honest words of peace?
>
> Will he keep the treaty of [Esarhaddon, king of Assyria]? Will he do [whatever i]s pleasing to Esarhaddon, king of Assyria?[27]

This inscription is quite interesting, for Bartatua sends an ambassador to fetch one of Esarhaddon's daughters for marriage. Esarhaddon asks the god Shamash if it is even worth handing over a daughter. The reason is not so much that Bartatua is a barbarian, but rather, will he keep his oath or peace if Esarhaddon agrees. One of two issues in the realm of war and diplomacy is visible regarding this inscription. The first is diplomacy. The tribe of Scythians led by Bartatua is strong enough to pose a real threat to Assyria's security and the offer is worthy of consideration by Esarhaddon. The second is political, suggesting a past collaboration of a once firm, yet cautious, relationship between Assyria and the various Scythian and Cimmerian tribes before the debacle with Sargon II.

Besides the political debate a question still looms, did Esarhaddon hand over his daughter to Bartatua? No one is positive that Esarhaddon handed over his daughter

Šerua-etirat to Bartatua. This is not to say Esarhaddon did not marry her off to Bartatua, but there is no record she ever married him. No one is certain if Esarhaddon handed over any daughter in marriage to Bartatua.[28] Nevertheless, whether or not the marriage took place, the agreement between the two powers was established roughly around 672 BCE.[29]

The Assyrians and the Scythian people led by Bartatua shared a time of peace. It is possible that during the peace agreement, Esarhaddon used this strategic alliance with Bartatua as a means to secure his northeastern borders against other nomadic elements. This level of trust gave Esarhaddon a sense of security to the northeast of Assyria. With this security and trust depending on the agreement, Esarhaddon may have used Bartatua to conduct proxy wars, calling upon the Scythians under Bartatua to serve as auxiliaries when needed. Whatever the case may be, one thing is certain, Bartatua walked the political fence line between Urartu and Assyria, as other Scythian or Cimmerian chieftains had done before.

Scythians, Kastariti and the Coalition

Esarhaddon may have used Bartatua to help him deal with a new coalition that threatened Assyria's northeastern borders. A chieftain named Kastariti, identified as Phraortes, according to Herodotus, led this new threat, or so we think,[30] around 671 BCE.[31]

Esarhaddon had to deal with the same old recurring problem again, nomads. Various nomadic elements were on the march and began to threaten Assyria's northeastern border. Now, even though Esarhaddon possibly made an agreement, a peace treaty, and offered friendship with Bartatua the Scythian, there is a new and old threat on the horizon. Esarhaddon speaks of this new threat in a prayer:

> [Šamaš, great lord, give me a firm positive answer to what I am asking you]!
> [From this day, the 22nd day of this month, Sivan (III), to the 21st day of the following month, Tammuz (IV), of this year, for 30 days and nights], the stip[ulated term for the performance of (this) extispicy — within this stipulated term],
> will the troops of the S[cyth]ia[ns, which have been staying in the district of Mannea and which are (now) moving out from the territory] of Mannea, strive and plan?
> Will they move out and go through the passes [of Hubuškia] to the city Harrania (and) the city Anisus? Will they take much plunder and heavy booty from the territory of [Assyria]? Does your great divinity [know it]?[32]

This movement caught the attention of the Assyrian spies who dotted the Mannean landscape, sending back pieces of information for Esarhaddon to look over and consider as he consulted with his generals and gods. Esarhaddon considers the advice and rightly shows distrust of the Scythians. Nevertheless it is clear, this is no small Scythian movement, but rather large, if not overwhelming. This also tells us that these Scythians may not be the Scythians under the leadership of Bartatua. The identity of the leader is uncertain, but the movement is of enough concern and the information good enough to speculate on which route the Scythians will take if any attack on Assyria does take place.

Esarhaddon continues in this next inscription, praying to the god Samas for advice, asking if the Scythians will invade through the Hubuskian passes and plunder parts of Assyria. Esarhaddon's prayer and his information obtained from his spies, concerned him enough to take precautionary action, leading to questions about when and where the Scythians would attack, and if others would rise up to collude with them?

> [Šamaš, great lord, gi]ve m[e a firm positive answer to what I am asking you]!
> [Esarhaddon, king of Assyria, who is now intent] on sending a messenger [of his choice to NN, king of Hubuški]a, and (whom) [your great divinity] knows —

> [in accordance with the command of your great divinity, Šamaš, great lord, and yo]ur favo[rable decisions, should the subject of this query, Esarhaddon, king of Assyria, strive and] p[la]n, and [send his messenger to Hubuškia]?
> [If he, having planned, sen]ds (him), [his messenger, whom he is sen]ding [to Hubuškia] —
> will [the Urarṭians, or the Cimmeri]ans, [or the Manne]ans, [or the Scythians, or the ...eans, o]r any other enemy [striv]e and plan, attack [that messenger, and seiz]e and kill him?[33]

Esarhaddon is compelled to do something quickly. He asks the gods for answers due to his concern for his messenger, as well as the important message. In other words, what is the attitude and atmosphere in the presence of the enemy, what news can the messenger bring back other than what he is told? Esarhaddon's prayers tell us something else: Assyria lives in fear of attack from the northeast, for Assyria is weak and losing its power and influence over its northern neighbors. But there is more to this inscription besides Esarhaddon questioning the Scythians intentions; he refers to them now as enemies. This is where it gets fuzzy. If Bartatua and Esarhaddon signed a peace pact, why is Esarhaddon referring to the Scythians as enemies?

Unfortunately, later inscriptions mentioning the Scythians do not mention Bartatua. This remains problematic and suggests that Bartatua and Esarhaddon never agreed to a peace deal, or if they did, the peace between the two lasted for a very short time. If one looks to the previous inscriptions speaking of the Hubuskian passes, taking into account that those passes are not far from Sakiz, where Bartatua dwelled, it becomes possible that Esarhaddon is referring to those Scythians led by Bartatua. However, his name remains silent, leaving us to conclude either that Bartatua is dead, or he is alive and uninvolved with the latest uprising.

Another interesting point to make about the two previous inscriptions is that both the Cimmerians and Scythians are mentioned alongside the Manneans. Either Bartatua is alive, taking part in this operation to attack Assyria, or his hands are clean and no thought of hostility exists between him and Assyria. What is possible is that the Cimmerians and Scythians are two different groups not associated with or loyal to Bartatua, but are hostile to Assyria with no visibly distinct leader.[34] Whether Bartatua was involved in helping or shaping this uprising against Assyria remains unknown, at least unknown until some scraps of information are found to fill up the void. Nevertheless, what is relevant is that the coalitions taking action are described in the two previous inscriptions, which mention Manneans, Scythians, and Cimmerians along with Urartians as being hostile towards Assyria. Esarhaddon questions and sends messengers to the king of

Hubuskia, whose name is not mentioned, but the tension begins to rise between the various factions hostile to Assyria. Then Esarhaddon questions the gods whether to send troops to a place known as Siriš:

> within this stipulated term, (should) Esarhaddon, king of Assyria, who is now intent on sending men, horses and troops, as he wishes, to Siriš, (and) whom your great divinity knows —
> in accordance with the command of your great divinity, Šamaš, great lord, (and) your favorable decisions, should the subject of this query, Esarhaddon, king of Assyria, strive and plan?
> Should he send men, horses and troops, as he wishes, to Siriš? Is it pleasing to your great divinity?
> If the subject of this query, Esar[haddon], king of Assyria, having planned, sends (them), will the people of Siriš, or the Manneans, or the Ridaeans, or any (other) enemy, from this day to the day of my [stipu]lated term, band themselves together into an army (against) the army he is sending to [Siriš]?
> Will they [...] by their own [delibe]ration, strive and plan, and [attack the army of Esarh]addon, in order to kill,

plun[der, loot? Will they kill] what there is to k[ill, plunder what there is to plunder], loot [what there is to lo]ot in their midst [...]? Will it be delivered to them as booty?[35]

The tensions are high and Esarhaddon understands that if he does not send troops to Siriš, he will end up facing more trouble than he wishes to confront. It is possible Esarhaddon did send troops, but unfortunately, the rest of the tablet is broken. Whatever Esarhaddon decided, war was inevitable and it started at a place known as Dur-Illil.

The inscription suggests the Manneans made the first strike successfully by taking a place known as Dur-Illil, which is a city and fort on the Mannean border with Assyria. Esarhaddon begins to question the god Šamaš, asking what the enemy's intentions are and what to do about the situation,[36] questioning whether or not to send troops and if he did, would they be victorious.[37] Esarhaddon's prayer may indicate that Assyria was too weak to deal with the problem head on, but it is also possible that Esarhaddon is being cautious. Even though Mannean forces are attacking Assyria, there is no mention of the Cimmerians or Scythians fighting alongside the Manneans. Esarhaddon was being cautious, for if he had sent a rather large army to the northeast to punish the Mannean forces, the Scythians and Cimmerians could have made a surprise attack elsewhere, inasmuch as Esarhaddon questions their whereabouts and intentions, as indicated in previous inscriptions.[38]

The Assyrians and Manneans are committed to combat after the capture of Dur-Illil by Mannean forces. The conflict to have been an isolated incident, but the implications were far greater and the Assyrians understood this well. Nevertheless, one should not read this as a conflict between established kingdoms, but a conflict of the irritated. This irritation would bring forth the myriads of nomadic peoples who roamed Assyria's northeastern borders.

Shortly after the Mannean attack took place, Esarhaddon begins focusing on the whereabouts and intentions of the Scythians and Cimmerians:

> will] the tro[ops of the Scythians (and) the troops of the Cimmerians] emerge [from] the pass [of ... and go to Bit-Hamban and Parsumaš, will they make a dangerous incursion into the district of ...] and the district of [Šamaš-naṣir],
>
> will they loot [......]?
>
> [Is it decreed and confirmed] in a favorable case, by the command [of your great divinity, Šamaš, great lord]? Will he who can see, see it? [Will he who can hear, hear it]?

[(whether) they will make] a dangerous [incursion] to the dist[rict of Šamaš-naṣir, kill, plunder and loot].[39]

The inscriptions show a concern for the impending attack to come from the Scythians and Cimmerians, and yet describes how they are now officially at war with Assyria. The report to Esarhaddon suggests the Scythians and Cimmerians have been darting in and out of Assyria, making raids when and where they can with little if any resistance, before any real commitment to attack was to take place. In other words, the Scythians and Cimmerians were sending out feelers, checking for weak spots to take advantage of, such as the areas of Bit-Hamban[40] and Parsumaš,[41] both southeast of Nineveh and located in the Zagros Mountains.

    Because of the events taking place to Esarhaddon's east, he understood that looting might lead to conquest and subjugation of the areas affected. These nomadic entities were taking advantage of Assyria with ease. This suggests the Scythian and Cimmerian forces were looking to divert some of Assyria's forces from the north and northeast in order to spread them thinly against future attacks. The Scythians and Cimmerians had made their way down the Zagros Mountains and were attacking from the east or southeast rather than from the northeast. Nevertheless, we do not know the exact intention of these nomads, whether this was a coordinated attack or just random. However, due to the location of the raids and possible attempt to conquer the areas around the cities mentioned, the Scythians and Cimmerians seem to be helping a new host by the name of Kastariti, better recognized to us as Phraortes.

Kastariti or Phraortes, whichever you prefer, is a mysterious figure, for once again, what we do know about Kastariti is what we read in Herodotus and in the Assyrian inscriptions. Kastariti appeared on the scene around 671 BCE, according to the Assyrian texts.[42] The inscription you are about to read is the first time Kastariti is mentioned, along with another person named Mamitiaršu, who was a city lord of the Medes. Both men, particularly Kastariti, are conspiring to break away and challenge Assyria. This disturbs Esarhaddon, for besides the attack on his eastern border by the Scythians and Cimmerians, additional nomadic forces will soon be putting pressure on his eastern border. Esarhaddon begins to pray asking what his enemy's intentions are:

> [Šamaš, gre]at [lord], give [me] a firm positive answer to what I am asking you!
> [Kašt]aritu, city lord of Karkašsî, who wrote to Mamiti[aršu, a city lord] of the Medes, as follows: "Let us act together [and break away] from [Assyria]" —
> Will [Mami]tiaršu listen to him? Will he comply? Will he be pleased? Will he become hostile to Esarhaddon, king of

> [Assyria] this year? Does your great divinity [know it]?
>
> Is the [hosti]lity of Mamitiar[šu], a city lord of the Medes, [against Esarhaddon, ki]ng of Assyria, [decreed and confirmed] in a favo[rable case ......][43]

Esarhaddon now finds himself in a predicament, for many nomadic forces now or soon will be converging on Assyria. Esarhaddon shows his worry that if measures are not taken soon, the face of Assyria could change.

It is obvious that Kastariti is the leader of this coalition, even though the Assyrian texts mention another by the name of Mamitiaršu, with whom Kastariti wishes to associate himself, but whether the Cimmerians, Scythians, and Manneans jumped on board Kastariti's bandwagon remains unknown. The uprising instigated by Kastariti seems to be separate and in reaction to the events taking place along the eastern border of Assyria. In addition, he wishes to recruit Mamitiaršu for his cause, and he may have joined Kastariti in this rebellion against Assyria, but the problem is that future inscriptions fall silent concerning Mamitiaršu.[44] Nevertheless, this is not to say he did not join Kastariti' Assyrian inscriptions continue to mention the Medes without reference to Mamitiarsu.

> Will Kaštaritu with his troops, or the troops of the Cimmerians, or the troops of the

> Medes, or the troops of the Manneans, or any other enemy, strive and plan?[45]

This inscription and seven more to follow in the Assyrian texts refer to the Medes as an enemy of Assyria during this crisis, but only one inscription mentions a Mede by name as a city lord. This tells us Mamitiaršu is just one Median chieftain among many, and evidently was the first one to consider Kastariti's offer to align himself with the rebellion against Assyria.

The name Mede or Medes, mentioned in this next inscription by Esarhaddon, indicates that a wide-scale rebellion is now under way and suggests that the Medes had no central king or chieftain, but perhaps a coalition of local chiefs unified under Kastariti's banner. Nevertheless, this does not mean that the entire Median nation is at war with Assyria, only segments supportive of the cause. Media is just a region, not necessarily a nation of peoples united under a single ruler like Assyria. Esarhaddon uses the term Mede in a regional sense and rather generically:

> Kaštaritu, with [his troops, or the troops of the Cimmerians] or the troops of the Medes or [the troops of the Manneans, or any enemy will enter] that city, Ka[ribtu], conquer [that city, Karibtu, (and whether) it will be delivered to them].[46]

Esarhaddon repeatedly mentions and lumps the Cimmerians, Scythians, Manneans, and Medes together in this rebellion with no real distinction as to who is attacking or who will be attacking, as in the case of the city of Karibtu on the Assyrian border. However, the question remains, were the Scythians and Cimmerians going along with the various nomads helping Kastariti directly? Or was it a joint effort with little coordination in which the various nomads all agreed on their objective, which was Assyria? On the other hand, it is also possible none of these nomadic groups is ever in any type of coalition or joint effort in helping one another attack the Assyrian Empire. Rather, they may have heard of the rebellion and decided to join in the cause without ever coming face to face with the originators. How this conflict started remains clouded, but the Assyrian inscriptions do suggest a number of considerations and speculations.

In conclusion, concerning Kastariti and the environment of the rebellion described in the inscriptions, one can see that a gradual domino effect took place with certainty. Moreover, the Assyrian inscriptions lump the various nomadic tribes all into one. However, the Scythians, Cimmerians, and Manneans were in a somewhat loosely joined effort in attacking Assyria along with Kastariti and his forces. The rebellion was too big to go unnoticed by the other nomads; they would have worked together, even if they were at odds with one another. The nomadic enemies of Assyria seem not to be united in a collective front, but rather united in the collective cause, to topple or seriously wound the Assyrian Empire. To make a final note concerning Kastariti and his battles, it may be speculated that he did indeed attack and defeat Assyrian forces along with capturing Assyrian cities, or cities under Assyrian control that were not part of Assyria proper. The inscriptions mention him conquering the cities of Kišassu, Karibtu, Ṣubara, Ušiši, and Kilman.[47]

It does seem possible according to Esarhaddon's tone in the inscriptions that Kastariti did have success defeating the Assyrian military. From the political standpoint, Assyria lost its power of influence and control over these nomadic border defenders, but some stayed loyal to Assyria despite that many more rebelled. From the military standpoint, Assyria seems to have been overwhelmed by the sheer size of the forces working together against Assyria, but this is unlikely. What is more plausible than the numbers game is that the various tribes of nomads seem successful in weakening the Assyrian forces by spreading them thinly from the north to the south along Assyria's eastern border. In addition, these various groups demonstrated the ability to conduct siege warfare, like that of the Assyrians, which suggests many of these nomadic groups had formerly served as Assyrian auxiliary or received training from Assyria's enemies, like Urartu or Elam.[48]

The outcome remains unknown, since Esarhaddon does not speak much about his failures at the time, nor is there any indication of whether or not Kastariti died in battle or survived to fight another day, even though

Herodotus does tell us that Kastariti (Phraortes), "reigned over the Medes two-and-twenty years."[49] If this were the case, then he would have died in battle, according to Herodotus, under the reign of Ashurbanipal. One is at a loss, since the Assyrian tablets do not speak of a man named Phraortes, nor a battle he led against Ashurbanipal. Therefore, it seems the Phraortes Herodotus is speaking of is the one whom King Darius of Persia defeated during a revolt.[50]

Conclusion to Esarhaddon

Esarhaddon's rule over Assyria was not long and sweet. He had many friends, but many more enemies, among whom the worst and most annoying were the Scythians and Cimmerians. Esarhaddon understood these two groups would not go away any time soon, even after his death. With all his praying and questioning, he never gets a straight answer and instead lives in a limbo of concern. He may have won the battles or lost as many as he won, but he never won the war. Every time he defeated a Cimmerian or Scythian army, another would show up to replace the dead, rapidly pointing the spear towards Assyria's border. In a way, the Cimmerians and Scythians were like the Immortals of Persia. If you killed one, another one would take his place, and sometimes others joined in. In 669 BCE, Esarhaddon was preparing to campaign against the rebellious Egyptians, but it would not happen. He became ill en route and died in the city of Harran.[51]

"The twelfth year, the king of Assyria [marched on Misir]. On the way he fell ill and, in the month of Arah[samnu], the tenth [da]y, he went to his destiny. Esarhaddon reigned twelve years over Assyria. His two sons ascended the throne, Samas-suma-ukin in Babylon, Ashurbanipal in Assyria."[52]

Endnotes: Chapter Three

[1] Simo Parpola, *The Correspondence of Sargon II, Part I: Letters from Assyria and the West State Archives of Assyria, Volume I*, 1.
[2] Strabo *Geography*, 1.3.21
[3] Plutarch *On Superstition*, 8
[4] Herbert Jennings Rose, *Primitive culture in Greece* (Toronto: Methuen & Co. Ltd., 1925), 208.
[5] Thomas J. Haley, William O. Berndt, *Handbook Of Toxicology* (New York: Hemisphere Publishing Corporation, 1987), 5.
[6] Roger Pearse. "Jerome, Chronicle." Early Church Fathers - Additional Texts. www.tertullian.org/fathers/jerome_chronicle_02_part1.htm (accessed August 5, 2010).
[7] Rodney S. Young, *The Gordion excavations. 1. Three great early tumuli*, (Cambridge: University of Pennsylvania Museum of Archaeology and Anthropology, 1982), 272.
[8] DeVries, Keith, Peter Ian Kuniholm, G. Kenneth, and Sams & Mary M. Voigt. "New dates for Iron Age Gordion." Antiquity. www.antiquity.ac.uk/projgall/devries296/ (accessed August 7, 2010).
[9] Leick, 57.
[10] H.W.F. Saggs, *The Might that was Assyria*, (London: Sidgwick & Jackson, 1984), 106-107.
[11] Leick, *Who's who in the Ancient Near East*, 137.
[12] King James Bible
[13] Boris Piotrovsky, *The Ancient Civilization of Urartu* (New York: Cowles Book Co, 1969), 126-130.
[14] Ivantchik, 155.
[15] Sir E. A. Wallis Budge, *The History of Esarhaddon: Son of Sennacherib King of Assyria, 1880. Reprint* (New York: Kessinger Publishing, 2005), 45.
[16] Edwin Norris, *Assyrian Dictionary: Intended to further the study of the cuneiform inscriptions of Assyria*, vol. II (Paris: Adamant Media Corporation, 2004), 403.
[17] Norris, *Assyrian Dictionary: Intended to further the study of the cuneiform inscriptions of Assyria*, vol. II, 628.
[18] Ivantchik, 155.
[19] Iorwerth Eiddon and Stephen Edwards, *The Cambridge Ancient history, Volume 3, Part 1* (Cambridge: Cambridge University Press, 1969), 358.
[20] Ivan Starr, *Queries to the Sungod: Divination and Politics in Sargonid Assyria*, 23.

[21] Drews, 114.
[22] E. Raymond Capt, *Missing Links Discovered in Assyrian Tablets* (Thousand Oaks, CA: Artisan Sales, 1985), 119-120.
[23] E. A. Wallis Budge, *The History of Esarhaddon: Son of Sennacherib King of Assyria BC 681 to 668* (Whitefish, MT: Kessinger, 2005), 45-47.
[24] Herodotus, *The Histories* 1. 103.
[25] Sulimirski and Taylor, *Cambridge Ancient History, Vol III/2* (Cambridge: Cambridge University Press, 1991), 564–565.
[26] Roman Ghirshman, *Iran from the earliest times to the Islamic conquest* (Baltimore: Penguin Books, 1961), 106-107.
[27] Starr, *Queries to the Sungod: Divination and Politics in Sargonid Assyria*, 20.
[28] Radner, Karen. "Knowledge and Power - The royal family: queen, crown prince, eunuchs and others." Knowledge and Power - Knowledge and Power in the Neo-Assyrian Empire. http://knp.prs.heacademy.ac.uk/essentials/royalfamily/ (accessed September 16, 2010).
[29] Ivantchik, 93.
[30] Herodotus, *The Histories* 1. 102.
[31] Ivantchik, 92.
[32] Starr, *Queries to the Sungod: Divination and Politics in Sargonid Assyria*, 23.
[33] Ibid., p. 24
[34] Hermann . Sauter, "9.2.1.4 Comments on the "coalition" against Assyria." Studies on Kimmerier problem. http://translate.google.com/translate?hl=en&sl=de&tl=en&u=http%3A%2F%2Fwww.kimmerier.de%2Fstart.htm (accessed December 23, 2010).
[35] Starr, 24-28.
[36] Ibid, 29-31.
[37] Ibid, 33-34.
[38] Ibid, 23-24.
[39] Ibid, 35-37.
[40] Otto Edzard Dietz, Encyclopaedia of Assyriology and Near Eastern Archaeology (RLA) - Volume 9 (Berlin: W. de Gruyter 2001), 91-92.
[41] K. E. Eduljee. "Parsa, Persia. Page 2. Early Achaemenian History, Parsumash, Parsamash, Parsa. c 700-560 BCE.." Heritage Institute - Corporate Governance, Institutional Governance. http://www.heritageinstitute.com/zoroastrianism/achaemenian/page2.htm (accessed April 14, 2011).

[42] Ivantchik, 92.
[43] Starr, 41.
[44] Ibid.
[45] Ibid, 43.
[46] Ibid, 44.
[47] Ibid, 43-44, 48-51.
[48] Ilya Gershevitch, *The Cambridge History of Iran, Volume 2: The Median and Achaememian Periods*, 105-106.
[49] Herodotus, *The Histories* 1. 102.
[50] Cam Rea, *Isaac's Empire: Ancient Persia's Forgotten Identity* (Shelbyville, KY: Wasteland Press, 2009), 57.
[51] Roux, 329.
[52] Jean Glassner and Benjamin Foster, *Mesopotamian Chronicles* (USA: Society of Biblical Literature, 2004), 203.

4

Ashurbanipal's Hell

Ashurbanipal's reign began in 668 BCE without challenge to the throne. His grandmother, Queen Naqi'a-Zakuta, made anyone affiliated with the Assyrian court to swear an oath of loyalty that Ashurbanipal was the rightful heir. When King Ashurbanipal took the throne, he inherited the problem of rebellions that his father previously had fought within and without the empire.

In 667 BCE, he sent a stronger army to put down the rebellion in Egypt and retook the city of Memphis. In doing so, Pharaoh Necho I was placed on the throne of Egypt with the Assyrian army backing his claim.[1] A little after the events in Egypt took place, sometime around the 660's BCE, a rider came from a far-away land with a message in writing. None of the King's officials had ever heard or read his language and had to find someone who could interpret it. The visitor's letter was from Gyges of Lydia. It was a plea to Ashurbanipal for military assistance against an old-time foe, the Cimmerians. Ashurbanipal immediately prayed to his god Shamash, asking what the wisest course of action would be in dealing with yet another Cimmerian problem:

Gyges' rider set out [...]. He reached the border of my country. My men spotted him and asked him: "Who are you, stranger, you, whose country's rider never traveled the road to the frontier?" They brought him [...] to Nineveh, my royal city, into my presence. But of all the languages of east and west, over which the god Aššur has given me control, there was no interpreter of his tongue. His language was foreign, so that his words were not understood.[2]

Once an understanding was established, the Assyrians understood the problem, and the problem was Cimmerians. Previously, we touched on the Cimmerians invading and overrunning parts of Anatolia during the reign of Esarhaddon. These Cimmerians had not left the area and caused the kings of Lydia, Cilicia, and Tabal to request help from Assyria in dealing with the Cimmerian situation.[3]

Gyges was most likely delighted to hear the news that Assyria would assist him against the Cimmerians. In 665 BCE, the Lydians under King Gyges defeated the Cimmerians with Assyrian support. In showing his appreciation for Assyria's help, Gyges sends Ashurbanipal a few trophies:

Gyges, king of Lydia (Gūgu šar māt Luddi) a district by the passes of the sea,

a distant place, whose name the kings, my ancestors, had not heard, the god Ashur, my begetter, revealed word of my kingship to him in a dream:

"Ashurbanipal, king of Assyria, the beloved of Ashur, king of the gods, lord of all—Lay hold of his princely feet!

Revere his sovereignty, Implore his rule. As obeisance and tribute-bearing, let your prayers come before him.

By invoking his name, conquer your enemies!" On the (very) day he had this dream, he dispatched his rider to inquire of my well-being.

Through his messenger, he sent to relate to me the dream that he had. From the day he laid hold of my royal feet the Cimmerians (Gimirrāya) (who) harass his countrymen, a wicked enemy, who had never honored my ancestors or me, had never laid hold of my royal feet, he captured alive in the midst of battle with the aid of Ashur, Marduk, Ishtar, the gods, my lords.

Out of the Cimmerian village heads which he captured, two village

> heads he put in handcuffs, iron manacles, shackles and iron fetters, and together with his rich gifts, to Nineveh, my capital, he sent into my presence.
>
> He kissed my feet.
>
> (Thus) I experienced the might of Ashur and Marduk.[4]

What started well between the two powers was based on a mutual hatred and concern for the Cimmerians, but this would end between the two when Gyges sent Carian and Ionian hoplites to aid Tushamilki, who happened to be the king of Musur.

During the early stages of Ashurbanipal's rise to power and before Gyges fell from Ashurbanipal's favor, Ashurbanipal mentions a king of Tabal named Mugallu:

> Mugallu, king of the Tabal, who had harassed the kings my fathers, brought [(his) daughter, his own offspring, with great dowries to Nineveh to be a lady-in-waiting; he kissed my feet. As for Mugallu, I imposed on him great horses as annual payment.[5]

This inscription speaking of Mugallu, dated roughly around the 660's BCE, may refer to the time when Gyges, king of Lydia, made an alliance with Assyria. Whatever the case may be, this inscription tells us Mugallu was caught between two powers and had many options to consider. Remember, Tabal was closer to Assyria than Lydia, but was much closer to the Cimmerians and Scythians, who had hegemony over the Syrian region that bordered his own kingdom.[6]

From what one can gather, Mugallu apparently feared Assyria much more. Sending gifts and a daughter as a peace offering in order to avoid Assyrian invasion seemed to be the best option. Mugallu may have made the right choice, for his other options seem to be much more dangerous. If Mugallu stayed neutral, he was stuck between Assyria, Lydia, and the powers allied with the two. Because of this choice, he was threatened by not only Assyria and Lydia, but also by the Cimmerian and Scythian factions. These might have pressured Mugallu into sending a messenger to Ashurbanipal's court, to seek an alliance by subjecting his kingdom and making apologies for past occurrences.[7] Mugallu could have tried to ally with the Cimmerians and Scythians, as he may have done before. He may have realized they were loosely organized, altough well equipped, but more importantly, their loyalty was fleeting.[8]

With Assyria and those allied now loosely secured from western intrusions conducted by the various Cimmerian and Scythian factions, the same can be said concerning the eastern portion of the Assyrian Empire. With that said, these alliances may in fact have allowed Ashurbanipal to be comfortable and cautious enough to invade the province of Mannea in 660 BCE without worrying about attack by the Cimmerian and Scythian elements that held a hegemony over the Syrian region at the time.[9]

In 660 BCE, Ashurbanipal invaded the province of Mannea. The Mannaeans, led by Ahseri with possible Scythian or Cimmerian help, attacked Assyrian forces in Zumua, located in the Zagros Mountains. Ashurbanipal had to respond with force, for the Zagros Mountains had deteriorated and were overrun, most likely by a vast element of nomadic peoples, such as the Scythians, Cimmerians, Medes, and whoever else rode on a horse and carried a bow.[10] Ashurbanipal said:

> In my fourth campaign I mobilized my troops and took the straightest way against Ahseri, the king of Mannea. Upon the command of Assur, Sin, Samas, Adad, Bel, Nabu, Istar of Nineveh, the Lady of Kidmuri, Istar of Arbela, Ninurta, Nergal, and Nusku I entered Mannea and triumphantly marched through it. I conquered, devastated, destroyed and burned with fire its fortified cities and its numberless small towns as far as Izirtu. The people, horses, donkeys, bulls and sheep I removed from the cities and counted them among the booty.
>
> Ahseri, when he heard my troops coming, left Izirtu, his royal residence. He

fled to Istatti, his stronghold, and sought shelter there. I conquered this area, devastated a stretch of fifteen days' march and brought about a deathly silence. Istar, who dwells in Arbela, delivered Ahseri, who did not fear my lordship, up to his servants, according to the word that she had said in the very beginning: "I will, as I said, take care of the execution of Ahseri, the King of Mannea." The people of his country rose in rebellion against him, threw his corpse on the street of his city, dragging his body to and fro. With weapons they beat his brothers, his family and his kinsmen down. Afterwards his son Ualli ascended his throne. He acknowledged the authority of Assur, Sin, Samas, Adad, Bel, Nabu, Istar of Nineveh, the Queen of Kidmari, Istar of Arbela, Ninurta, Nergal, Nusku, the great gods, my lords, and submitted to my yoke. For the sake of his life he opened his hands and implored my lordship. His crown prince Erisinni he sent to Nineveh where he kissed my feet. I was merciful to him and sent to him an envoy of peace. He had a daughter of his own offspring brought to me to be my housekeeper. His former tribute that he had interrupted in the time of the kings, my fathers, was brought to me again. I added thirty horses to his former tribute and imposed them on him.[11]

Not only did Ashurbanipal seek to punish the Mannaeans, he also attacked the western Medes around 659 BCE, capturing seventy-five towns during the campaign.[12] Ashurbanipal might not have been able to conduct these operations against Mannae and the Medes, had not his western flank been secured through alliances.

Now as mentioned earlier, Gyges had sent Carian and Ionian hoplites to aid Tushamilki around 655 BCE.[13] Tushamilki, king of Musur, (whom some identify as Pharaoh Psammetichos of Egypt) was a previous instigator of rebellion against the Assyrians. Ashurbanipal was so furious, he says:

> His messenger whom he kept sending to me to bring me greetings, he suddenly discontinued... he sent his forces to the aid of Tushamilki king of Musur, who had thrown off the yoke of my sovereignty. I heard of it, and prayed to Assur and Ishtar, saying, 'May his body be cast before his enemy, may his foes carry off his limbs.' The Cimmerians, whom he had trodden underfoot by calling upon my name, invaded and overpowered the whole of his land.[14]

I have changed the text of the inscription above, using "Musur" in place of "Egypt." I understand there are those who use Musur as indicating Egypt. If we use the term Egypt, even this can be misleading, because there is another country rendered as Musur to the north, next to the province of Que in southeastern Anatolia, which is Mizraim. It is rendered the same way Egypt is rendered in Hebrew. In addition, the name Tushamilki is not Egyptian, but is a Semitic name, probably Phoenician. Furthermore, when looking at Ashurbanipal's first campaign, he went into combat with Ahumilki, king of Ashdod and Milkiashapa, king of Byblos. Looking at some of his father's campaigns, you will notice he fought people such as Adbimilkutte, king of Sidon. All these names and many others are personal names with the letters "mlk" found in them. In Hebrew, as an example, "melek" means "king."

As mentioned, Gyges sent Carian and Ionian hoplites to aid Tushamilki around 655 BCE. It would not make much sense for Gyges to send troops to aid Egypt in the act of rebellion, when all the names mentioned were Semitic and their origin Phoenician, unless the king of Egypt was Phoenician, but this is unlikely. Moreover, it also would have been costly for Gyges to send in troops. More likely Gyges needed his troops to stay and defend his homeland and to move short distances to help aid other allies. However, if Gyges moved troops to Egypt, he would expose his northern flank to the Cimmerians and his eastern flank to the Assyrians. But if Gyges moved his troops east to Musur, this would be a short distance from his home base of operations, to which he could come back quickly in the event of a Cimmerian raid.

Gyges' rebellion against Assyria was due to Assyrian aggression. Ashurbanipal was just as much a threat as the Cimmerians. This may be the reason why Gyges had to send troops to Musur. Gyges understood that he had to make a stand, letting the Assyrians know that expansion towards his realm was not welcome. But because of this act of aggression against Assyria, Ashurbanipal wanted Gyges dead.[15]

How Gyges died remains shrouded in mystery. Nevertheless, Ashurbanipal gives us a clue:

> May his body be cast before his enemy, may his foes carry off his limbs. The Cimmerians, whom he had trodden underfoot by calling upon my name, invaded and overpowered the whole of his land.[16]

Notice in the inscription that Ashurbanipal says, "May his body be cast before his enemy, may his foes carry off his limbs." Some suggest Gyges died in battle against the Cimmerians around 652 BCE.[17] However, it is also likely, according to the inscription above, that Gyges did not die in battle, but in fact died from some unknown cause, for the inscription says his body is cast and his limbs spread about. This suggests that Gyges is already dead and buried when the Cimmerians rampaged throughout his kingdom, sacking Sardis around 650-645 BCE during the reign of Ardys II.[18] The Cimmerian effect caused Ardys to ask for forgiveness and help from Ashurbanipal:

> (Ardys the son of Gyges) grasped my royal feet, saying: 'You are the king whom the God cares for; you cursed my father, and misfortune was his share; but bless me, your obedient servant, so that I may pull the yoke of you(r chariot).[19]

This produces another question for your consideration concerning the Cimmerian invasion of Lydia. Did Ashurbanipal buy the services of the Cimmerians in order to pay back the Lydians for their support of Musur? The question is unanswerable, but the idea of paying one to punish another is conceivable.

Now, with Gyges out of Ashurbanipal's thoughts and prayers, this Cimmerian invasion of Lydia was much more dangerous than the Assyrians may have understood. The Cimmerians conducting the rampage seem much stronger and possibly better organized than before, for the man leading these Cimmerians will cause great worry and concern among the Assyrian people, particularly Ashurbanipal.

Dugdammi: King of the World

The Assyrians were already facing problems other than the Scythians and Cimmerians to the northeast of Assyria and to the west in Anatolia. This specific issue was regional and internal. Ashurbanipal had many problems even after conquering or putting down rebellions in Babylonia, Elam, and Egypt. Assyria was not in a position to take on more problems after a failed policy of economic aid to those affected by their own hand, which led in turn to brutish subjugation of the rebels, such as when Assyria sacked Elam sometime around the mid-640's BCE.[20]

Besides the events transpiring in and around Assyria of a non-nomadic nature, the Cimmerians were on the move again, but seemed to be in greater numbers than in the past. Assyria's new threat was slowly materializing on their northwestern and northeastern border. As mentioned before, these groups were typically unorganized and insufficient to pose a real threat other than hit-and-run guerilla tactics, and on some rare occasions, as you read earlier, joining in a battle. It is possible that this new Cimmerian-Scythian threat was loosely united, but by and large they did not mix, only getting involved in the affairs of the region they jointly controlled or roamed. Assyria at the time had no real control over Anatolia or Media. These two regions could be considered Assyria's blind spot. In this blind spot, a certain chieftain would rise up to become not only a king of the Cimmerians, but also the "king of the world." His name was Dugdammi.

The origin of Dugdammi is rather vague according to most historians, but we will try to discover the facts. His name in classical Greek was Lygdamis,[21] in Assyrian it was either Dugdammi or Tugdammi. He was either a Cimmerian or Scythian, since the names are interchangeable and are practically the same. His story begins around 660 BCE.[22] It seems that the first known attacks from Dugdammi were against Greek coastal cities such as Sardis of Lydia. Afterward, he pushed at the Assyrian empire around 652 BCE.[23] Because of this external pressure, Assyria would be drawn into another war against Urartu and Dugdammi's forces. Ashurbanipal mentioned Dugdammi in his annuals as "King of the Sakai and Qutu." The term Sakai (Scythians) was used primarily by Western Iranians to indicate those who spoke in the Iranian vernacular.[24]

Before we discuss Dugdammi and his effect on Assyria, we should focus on the various names mentioned such, as Sakai and Qutu.

The term Qutu, also rendered as Quti, Qutians, or even Gutium, is a loosely used generic and archaic expression during this period of Assyrian history that has no real value for identifying a particular people. The term Gutium when used by Ashurbanipal refers to those who were hostile to Assyria, particularly those who lived along the Zagros Mountains. However, the term was also applied to Manneans or Medes during this period. In other words, the term Gutium indicates anyone who is hostile and lives from east of the Tigris River into lands of Western Iran.[25] Therefore, it seems evident that when Ashurbanipal speaks of Dugdammi, he is telling us that Dugdammi is from the region of Gutium, which could mean that he came from Media or maybe from the province of Mannea. What is certain is that Dugdammi is King of the Sakai, while his base of operations is evidently in the lands of Gutium.

There are two interesting letters given to Ashurbanipal by his astrologer Akkullanu that discuss revelations about the origins of the Cimmerians, Scythians, and Umman-manda:

> To the king, my Lord, your slave Akkullanu. Peace be with the king, my Lord, may Nabu and Marduk bless the king, my Lord. March was visible on the path of the (stars) of Enlil, close to the feet of Persee; he/it was drab and pallid. I saw (it) the 26th day of the month of Aiaru, when it had risen strongly. I sent its interpretation later to the king, my Lord."[If] March approaches from Persee, there will be revolt in the Amurru country, the brother will kill his brother. The sovereign's palace will be robbed, the treasures of the country will be carried away to another country. The sign of the

country is unfavorable. The king of the world will be delivered by his gods to his enemy." It is a bad omen for the Amurru country. Your Assur gods (and), your god, will surely remove the power acquired by the Cimmerians, so great that it is, and will give it to the king, my Lord." ["If] the starry Sanuma approaches of the Enmesarra god, the heart of the country will be happy, [the people will increase."] Sanuma is March. [It is] a good omen for the king, my Lord. "So March rises while changing its color and if its radiance is yellow, the king of Elam will die this year." "So Nergal is small and pallid at the time of its apparition and that he changes his color strongly like a celestial star, he will be understanding for Akkad. The forces of my army will resist and undo the enemy. The enemy's army won't resist against my army. The livestock of Akkad will lie down quietly on grazing. The sesame and the dates will be abundant. The gods will be understanding for Akkad." "So March is visible in the month of Aiaru, some hostile actions will take place, (there will be) the defeat of Umman-manda." Umman-manda are the Cimmerians.

What is interesting about this letter is that Akkullanu is referring to the Amurru as Umman-manda, but he goes on to reveal that the Umman-manda is the Cimmerians. But what does this mean? It means that the term Amurru in this inscription tells us that the Umman-manda and the Cimmerians are the same and that they are Amurru. If this is true, then the Cimmerians and Scythians are originally from the lands west of Mesopotamia.[26]

The term Amurru in Akkadian means, "the west lands" or the land west of Mesopotamia which includes the Mediterranean coast.[27] The Assyrians are notorious for using archaic terms when referring to peoples who inhabit certain regions, such as the region of Syria, which would be a province within the lands of the Amurru and over which, as discussed earlier, the Scythians had hegemony.[28] On the other hand, Dugdammi's title, "King of the Sakai and Qutu" may refer to tribal identity and location of the residence, as previously mentioned.[29] If this is the case, then one should consider that the Cimmerians and Scythians came from the lands west of Assyria originally.

As for the term Umman-manda, the Assyrians and Babylonians have equated the Umman-manda with the Medes as described in the *Fall of Nineveh Chronicle*.[30] Moreover, the meaning of Umman-manda could be "Manda-host" or "host of the Manda." It has also been suggested that Umman-manda could mean "Who Knows," "Barbarous people," or "Nomads." Nevertheless, one could say that the term means nothing more than a mixed multitude of uncivilized people from the north.[31]

The meaning of the term Umman-manda has evolved among the regional people that mentioned them. Take for instance the name Tidcal or Tudkhul. Tidcal/Tudkhul is said to be the king of the Hittites, but he is also called king of the Umman-manda or "Nations of the North."[32] Consider also a much older event in which Naram-Sin, king of the Akkadian empire, defeated the Umman-manda and he states, "the powers of the Umman-manda are struck down."[33]

So what does this mean? This means from the time the Umman-manda first were mentioned by Naram-Sin up to the time of Ashurbanipal, over a thousand years had elapsed between events.[34] This suggests that the term Umman-manda is generic and does not identify one particular people, but rather a horde of many tribes with various names, and Ashurbanipal's Umman-manda are the Cimmerians. Therefore, the term Umman-manda was just a Mesopotamian stereotype used when referring to people not native to the civilized powers in the region. The Umman-manda of Naram-Sin and the Umman-manda of Ashurbanipal were indeed two different peoples.

The next interesting aspect of this letter indicates that Dugdammi is not only king but also king of the world, for the letter states, "The King of the world will be delivered by his gods to his enemy." The Assyrians saw King Dugdammi worthy to hold the title "Sar kissati," which means "King of the universe"[35] or "King of the world" which is translated as "King of Kish."[36] This does not mean Dugdammi used the title or even considered the title, let alone even knew about the title, but rather that the Assyrians found him worthy of the title. The meaning of the title "Sar kissati" suggests that Dugdammi controlled regions rather than smaller provinces. In ancient times, this title went to those who controlled vast regions within or outside the boundaries of Mesopotamia. Akkullanu tells Ashurbanipal that he will gain back the power and title once King Dugdammi is defeated. It seems that if Ashurbanipal defeats Dugdammi, he will gain back the respect of his people, as well as his enemy, and in doing so, he will control the four corners of the known world.[37]

Since there could only be one king of the world, Ashurbanipal of Assyria desired the title. Ashurbanipal was most likely envious that Dugdammi, a man of non-Assyrian birth, held such a prestigious and sacred title. Ashurbanipal desired the title for it meant the defeat of his regional rival and would secure Assyria's borders. The title Dugdammi holds brings up another question. The title "Sar Kassati," as discussed earlier, suggests that his domain would have been vast, extending from Anatolia to Western Iran if not further to the east. This would mean that Dugdammi was the first Cimmerian-Scythian king to rule, unlike his predecessors, who were mere chieftains. However, this is only speculation. For how extensive his nomadic empire may have been is a matter of debate, but to the Assyrians it was rather threatening.

Another interesting name comes from the next letter provided by Akkullanu to Ashurbanipal concerning a people known as the Ahlamu:

> ["So to him] month of Simanu [the moon] appears (for the first time) on 30th day (of Aiaru), the Ahlamu will eat the wealth of the Amurru country". [These] omens are bad for Amurru. [Assour, Be] Nabu, your gods, [if hostility,] to the king's hands, my Lord [...] [... the defeat] of your ene[mies[...] [...]³⁸

Once again, we notice the name Amurru being used which was shown previously to apply to the Cimmerians. Now we have the name Ahlamu added to the list as eating the riches of the Amurru. What is fascinating about this inscription is the Ahlamu are now side by side with Amurru as in olden times. The Ahlamu were a tribe of Arameans who were semi-nomadic and occupied northern Syria, many times giving Assyria trouble during the reign of Tiglath-pileser I around the 12th-11th centuries BCE.³⁹ The Ahlamu gave the Amurru people trouble during Biblical times, as well, for the people living within the lands of southern Syria and Canaan or any inhabitant who lived west of the Euphrates River, were considered Amurru by the Assyrians.⁴⁰ An example of this trouble is illustrated in I Chronicles 18:1-17, in which King David slew many Arameans.⁴¹ In other words, we have what the Assyrians would consider Amurru, that is Israel, and this is not due to ethnicity, but that Israel lives in the region designated by the Assyrians as Amurru country at the time. But what does this say about the Cimmerians and the

Ahlamu? The answer to that question is difficult but within reach. The Cimmerians under Dugdammi seem to have origins in Amurru country, but further investigation is needed due to the wording of the inscriptions.

Now, the letter or inscription you read says, "the Ahlamu will eat the wealth of the Amurru country." This seems to indicate that the Ahlamu are living within the confines of Dugdammi's empire and may be hostile to the Cimmerians, as indicated by eating the wealth of the Amurru. The Assyrians would know this due to their vast spy network and hoped the Ahlamu would cause a revolt significant enough to allow the Assyrians to take advantage of the situation. However, only two letters mention the Ahlamu as having a possible effect on the Cimmerians, but nothing more is mentioned other than possible hope. Ashurbanipal's inscriptions for some time would continue referring to Dugdammi as "the king of Amurru" without mentioning his name:

> The king of Amurru will die, his country will be reduced (in size) or again it will be devastated. The experts will probably have something to say about Amurru to the king my lord.[42]

> On the 15th day of Tebet, during the middle watch, a lunar eclipse took place: it began in the East and passed toward the West: a sinister omen, whose evil (import) is

confined to Amurru and its territory. (Indeed) it portends evil to the king of Amurru and to his country. Since the chief enemy of the king my lord is in Amurru, the king my lord may do as he wishes: the arms of the king my lord shall conquer, the king shall accomplish his defeat. The text of their decision is reliable: Shamash and Marduk are giving into the hands of the king my lord a passage through the land, which you have seized by force of arms, from the upper to the lower sea. From the shore of the sea I lift up my hands toward the king my lord, for you are benign. May Marduk and Sarpanitum intercede for me before the king my lord.[43]

Ashurbanipal must have been happy with his spy's reports that the soothsayers used to fill the king's ears with prophetic victory fast approaching. This also suggests the Assyrians may have become strong enough to make a challenge, thus giving Ashurbanipal the confidence to approach his enemy. Whatever reason allowed Ashurbanipal to feel more secure about his position seems to have backfired, for Dugdammi goes on to threaten the Assyrian border along with Mugallu's son, "ussi."

The name of Mugallu's son remains unknown, all that is left of his name on the inscription is "-ussi." This ussi along with Dugdammi would attack Assyria, but the outcome of the battle remains undecided:

> [x x] ussi, his son sent every year, without interruption his heavy tribute and implored [my] lordship. I made him swear by the great gods, my Lords, he (but) despised the oath by their (sic) great gods. He has conferred with Dugdammi, king of the barbarian destroyer? destructive. Assour, great mountain, whose signs / borders don't change, has it terrace [of] far and burned his body by the flaming fire. Without bow, nor horses, nor [mules], (nor?) his brothers, (nor?) his parent, seed of his father's house, his great army, the aid of his hands, sent emergency following his own decision of the horses and mules without number in Assyria. Dugdammi, king highlander (?), Gutium, insolent that didn't know the terror of Assour, has trusted in his own strength and has gathered his army to wage fight and battle. He established his camp on the border of Assyria. Assour, Ellilitu, Beautiful, Nabu, Ishtar living in Arbela [...] Blood flowed out of his mouth and its sick tomb. Following it [the fire of the sky has fallen on them (the Cimmerians), and himself, his army and his camp, he burned

them. Dugdammi was terrified, he is in a deplorable situation and removed his army and his camp; he came back... in his country. The terror of Assour, of Ellilitu, of Beautiful, of Nabu, of Ishtar of Arbela, gods who help me in striking him and he sent his captains (to establish) friendship and peace. I received [his heavy tribute]. Gold, multicolored clothes [...] with great horses [...horses of horsemanship of his lordship, military equipment, his heavy tribute, he sent it to me and he has kissed my feet. I made him swear to Assour and Ellilitu not to sin against the borders of the Assyria, and I have reinforced (it) while concluding with him a treaty under oath. He hasn't respected the bill under oath by the great gods. He has entered in the borders of Assyria with the intention to make pain [...]. He sinned against the borders of Assyria on the place of libation; for the establishment [...The weapon] of Assour, my Lord has stricken him; he became a madman, and in (his) madness he bit his fingers.[44]

From this inscription, we gather that Mugallu's son ussi was loyal for some time to Assyria but did go on to join Dugdammi and his forces. Some have suggested that ussi was pressured by Dugdammi's power. This is plausible, for ussi would feel pressured to make a decision based on the interest of his kingdom, since Dugdammi was a much closer threat than Ashurbanipal.[45] In addition, consider also that ussi, like many others, grew tired of Assyrian dominance that imposed heavy tribute. Assyria would impose heavy tribute as a form of punishment to those that rebelled. It would perpetuate bad feelings, leading to further uprisings as in the case of ussi. Because of this, one could look at Dugdammi as a way out of Assyrian dominance. Dugdammi was not a threat, after all, but a blessing.

The next part in this inscription indicates a cease-fire. Ashurbanipal would impose heavy tribute on Dugdammi. Notice that in the inscription it says divine intervention defeated Dugdammi and his forces. This defeat could have come from another force but it is unclear. It may have been that Dugdammi's attacker could not beat him and so they had settled for a draw. Had Ashurbanipal really defeated Dugdammi, the title "Sar Kassati" would be his; however, Ashurbanipal did not trounce Dugdammi and the Assyrian soothsayers never mention the title, while the Assyrian spies report only hostility.

These next inscriptions are somewhat similar to the previous one, particularly the next one you are about to read.

Dugdammi, demon gallu, barbarian-destructor [...] that doesn't bring [the yearly tribute,] [has trusted in] his own strength, [covered] the country like an invasion of locusts. He has gathered [his army and] established [his] camp [on the border of Assyria...] [...]... the coming down (?) Assour, sin, [Shamash, Ishtar of] Nineveh, Ishtar of Arbela [...] Blood flowed out [of his mouth;] he is [sick tomb.] [...] size, established place (?)] [... the fire of the sky is tomb and himself, [his army and his camp,] it burned [them]. [Dugdammi] [was terrified and] he is put in [a deplorable situation; [he removed his army and his camp,] in Harsale [...]... [...] (of) his countries rebelled against him and [...] he has expired. He was in a bad place and [...] [..] he plotted against my gods in the inside of his army. [...] theirs. The terror of Assour, of Sin, of Shamash of Ishtar of Nineveh, of Ishtar of Arbela, [gods, my Lords,] that helped me, striking him; his captains (to establish) friendship and peace [...] with [great (?)] horses [...]horses of horsemanship of his lordship, [...]...military equipment, his heavy [tribute,] he sent it to me and he has kissed my feet. I made him swear by the great gods, [my Lords not to sin] against the borders of Assyria and I have reinforced (it) [while concluding with him the treaty under oath. He rejected the treaties under oath by the great gods and [didn't respect it.] He has entered in the borders of Assyria with the intention (to make) pain. He sinned against the borders of Assyria [on the place] of libation; for the establishment (?) [...The weapon of Assour, my Lord struck him; [he became a madman,] and in (his) madness he bit his fingers. [...] he has changed and has inflicted upon him a stern punishment. [The moist of sound (body) has been reached of paralysis,] a sharp pain has pierced his heart; [...] of him didn't have, his army [...] his penis was claw and was tomb. [...His life ended...][46]

The inscription starts with Dugdammi being described as a "demon gallu" we will address this description later. As for the rest of the inscription, notices that it is a rehash of the previous inscription until you reach the last few portions. These last few lines suggest Dugdammi died in battle, using the imagery of a "pierced his heart" or his "penis was claw and was tomb." Overall, the message is simple, Dugdammi is dead and shall no longer pose a threat to Assyria, but there is more:

> [I have] killed, I have changed [Dugdammi, the king of Ummanmanda, destructive-barbarian...][47]

> And Dugdammi, king of Umman-manda, creation of Tiamat, a species of gallu demon, despised the oath [by the gods] not to make crime, not to sin against the borders of my country; he didn't fear your great name that the Igigis [venerate.] To magnify your lordship and the power of your divinity [...] Following the message of your divinity that you sent: "I will disperse [his] army [...] will I hurl down (?)] Sandakkurru / Sandaksatru, son (his), his offshoot that one designated like his heir." I heard (it) and I have glorified the powerful Marduk.[48]

Dugdammi is clearly dead according to the inscriptions, but another interesting aspect is the insults used to describe Dugdammi by Ashurbanipal. The term "demon gallu" and "Tiamat" as you read are descriptions of Dugdammi's character according to Ashurbanipal. The term "demon gallu" is in reference to seven demons who love to eat flesh.[49] You could take this meaning at face value, for some Scythian groups such as the Androphagoi and Massagetae did consume human flesh, and it is possible that Dugdammi partook of such a practice.[50] On the other hand, Dugdammi may not have consumed any human flesh, but rather his sword consumed the flesh of the many thousands he and his forces had slain. However, it could be a stereotype, for certain Scythians and Cimmerians may have partaken in the consumption of human flesh, while Dugdammi took no part in, but due to his relation to them, one would think otherwise. Nevertheless, whatever the circumstance is one can agree that the term shows the distaste Ashurbanipal had for Dugdammi and his nomadic forces.

The next term mentioned in the last inscription is "Tiamat." Tiamat represents the goddess of chaos. According to Babylonian mythology, Marduk slew Tiamat to create order and peace.[51] Ashurbanipal obviously saw himself as being in the same position as Marduk and that something had to be done in order to bring about social order. In other words, this war with Dugdammi was a clash of civilizations in Ashurbanipal's mind. You have the civilized Assyrians, keeping the peace and stability throughout the known world; while on the other hand, you have the uncivilized Dugdammi and his nomadic forces that represent palpable darkness.

The Assyrian inscriptions do not mention where Dugdammi died or how he died, but the statement is rather clear, Dugdammi is dead for, "a sharp pain has pierced his heart."[52] According to the historian Strabo, Dugdammi died at the Cilicia gates, but refers to him as Lygdamis and says, "Lygdamis, however, at the head of his own soldiers, marched as far as Lydia and Ionia and captured Sardes, but lost his life in Cilicia."[53] Unlike

Strabo's account, Ashurbanipal's letters do not mention where the battle took place but only mention Dugdammi's death. The inscriptions remain silent concerning a battle or a series of battles that most likely took place. However, the inscriptions do suggest a possible ceasefire at one time before the renewal of hostilities between the two.

The Ashurbanipal inscriptions mention two types of death; one is physical and the other spiritual. For the physical, Ashurbanipal says, "I have glorified the powerful Marduk."[54] Ashurbanipal claims the kill for himself, while in another inscription provided earlier speaks of the supernatural being responsible for slaying Dugdammi and says, "The weapon of Assour, my Lord struck him."[55] Regardless of the inscriptions, Ashurbanipal is responsible for Dugdammi's death. However, it is interesting that Ashurbanipal speaks of himself as the taker of life, while in other he speaks of a god having taken Dugdammi's life. It seems both are true, but with a twist.

To summarize, it is safe to say that Dugdammi was no friend of Assyria and he held in his grasp a huge nomadic empire that threatened the civilization of Assyria.[56] Before the hostilities began, it seems that a "soft alliance" existed between them, perhaps because Dugdammi had been bought off by Ashurbanipal in preparation for dismembering the kingdom of Lydia. If true, it would have been a great move by Ashurbanipal at the time, but the Cimmerians still proved too wild to control directly or indirectly, and they quickly turned their attention back toward Assyria. This turning could be due to the desperate plea for help of Ardys, son of Gyges, to Ashurbanipal, and his willingness to patch up their differences over past issues.

Ashurbanipal may have accepted the terms, which is a cause for concern. At this point, we could say that Dugdammi was still on comfortable terms with Assyria, but felt threatened and undermined by a possible new alliance between Ashurbanipal and Ardys.[57] The reason Ashurbanipal might have rekindled his trust in Lydia rather than with the Cimmerians could relate to economics and trade.

Lydia had an abundance of natural resources at its disposal, such as gold and silver. Trade routes also crossed through Lydia, making it and a commercial powerhouse for business and trade.[58] The fact is that Assyria needed resources such as iron ore. However, the Cimmerians that lived and roamed in the Anatolian region were also in control of the iron ore. The Cimmerians were bad for business and they had to go.[59] It seems that by making a pact with Lydia there was a chance to squeeze and expel the Cimmerians, as well as to establish trade relations with Lydia.

Earlier we discussed the death of Dugdammi and touched on the inconsistency of the battles, which suggest both Ashurbanipal and Dugdammi could have claimed victory. Both sides suffered heavy losses. However, it does seem that Ashurbanipal suffered most of the casualties in this conflict. Before the events that culminated in the death of Dugdammi, it appears that he took a short break before going on to violate the border agreement. This in turn would have caused upheaval along the borders and within Assyrian territory. In the inscriptions, one could glean from them that Ashurbanipal was quietly saying he was defeated. By invoking the god's name as the sole benefactor in defeating Dugdammi, it does suggest that an outside element was possibly responsible. This outside element may have been Madys, according to Strabo:

> Lygdamis, (King of the Cimmerians) however, at the head of his own soldiers, marched as far as Lydia and Ionia and captured Sardes, but lost his life in Cilicia. Oftentimes both Cimmerians and Trerans made such invasions as these; but they say that the Trerans and Cobus were finally driven out by Madys, the king of the Scythians. Let these illustrations be given here, inasmuch as they involve matters of fact which have a bearing upon the entire compass of the world in general.[60]

As Strabo suggests, it is quite possible that Madys did defeat and kill Dugdammi (Lygdamis) in Cilicia around 640 BCE[61] if not 639 BCE.[62] Ashurbanipal might have sent envoys to invite Madys to invade the lands of Dugdammi and kill him. The reason could be due to the wars in which Ashurbanipal was already engaged. Ashurbanipal was still intermittently fighting the Scythians and Cimmerians and ay the same time having to suppress rebellions in

Elam and Babylonia. Because of this, not only was he depleting his forces, he was also overextending his lines of supply and support. This massive onslaught on Assyria meant Ashurbanipal had to find someone to aid him, or hope for something or someone to intervene. He needed something as mighty as Dugdammi's forces in the north, whether it was by force or influence. Madys was the choice.[63] Strabo also says that Madys drove the Cimmerians out of Anatolia.[64] This could be true, but unlikely. Madys may have defeated the forces led by Dugdammi, but more likely, the dwindling remainder of Dugdammi's force simply joined Madys. This region was under Cimmerian control and they probably did not mind being ruled by one of their own kin.

Dugdammi did have a son by the name of Sandaksatru who would succeed Dugdammi after his death. However, nothing is really known about him or where he went. It is possible that Sandaksatru was with his father at Cilicia during the battle, and fled into Europe along with the remainder of the forces when his father was defeated and killed. Nevertheless, the inscriptions definitely make no mention of Sandaksatru's presence at this particular battle.[65]

Madyes, Cyaxares, and an Alternative

Madyes or Madys is another shadowy figure who steps onto the world stage. But who was Madyes and where did he come from? There is not a great deal of information about him, nor has his name turned up in any of the Assyrian tablets.[66] Herodotus and Strabo are the only two writers that mention him other than Arrian, who refers to him as "Idanthyrsus."[67]

Nevertheless, Herodotus provides the most information about Madyes. Most historians have read and used Herodotus' work for their research in dealing with this matter. But what if Herodotus was wrong? This would not be a new statement by any means nor is it to meant to demean Herodotus' work. So let us look at Herodotus' chronology from the Scythian invasion to the massacre of the Scythians by Cyaxares.

According to Herodotus, Madyes was the son of Bartatua (Protothyes)[68] but there is no concrete evidence for this even though some suggest he is the son of Bartatua and the Assyrian Princess.[69] Unfortunately, no evidence says Esarhaddon handed over his daughter in marriage. That is not to say it is not possible, but it has a high likelihood of being improbable.[70]

Herodotus tells us that Madyes "burst into Asia in pursuit of the Cimmerians whom they had driven out of Europe, and entered the Median territory."[71] This seems to be true to a certain extent, except for the fact that Madyes drove the Cimmerians from the battle into Europe rather than from Europe into Asia and not in the migratory sense. The sources provided by Herodotus and Strabo, along with Ashurbanipal's inscriptions, do attest that Dugdammi's defeat was by an outside element close to his borders and of the same ethnic stock, as both Herodotus and Strabo provide. Therefore, either Ashurbanipal paid for Madyes' services or it is true that Bartatua married an Assyrian princess to strengthen Assyrian-Scythian relations through Bartatua's son, Madyes. Madyes would become king of the Scythians and most likely was the nephew of Esarhaddon and cousin to Ashurbanipal, if this is true.

Now, Madyes was not king of all the Scythians, Umman-manda, or Cimmerians. However, it does seem that Madyes had a large army and possibly many provinces. His influence proved effective enough to sway Assyrian politics, as Bartatua had done to a certain degree. After Madyes took his father's throne, Ashurbanipal may have asked him to deal with Dugdammi. Thus, according to Herodotus, Madyes defeated and chased the remaining forces of Dugdammi out of Asia and into Europe.

Herodotus goes on to say, "The Scythians, having thus invaded Media, were opposed by the Medes, who gave them battle, but, being defeated, lost their empire. The Scythians became masters of Asia."[72] After Madyes effectively defeated Dugdammi in 639 BCE, he thus sets off to conquer the eastern half of Dugdammi's empire. The eastern half of Dugdammi's empire would be the regions of Media and Mannea. Thus, the Scythians under Madyes took full control of Dugdammi's empire. Therefore, to say, "The Scythians became masters of Asia" is incorrect and correct. It is incorrect to say the Scythians are the masters when they already had been, under Dugdammi, but it is correct to say the Scythians and other nomads have a new master by the name of Madyes.

The Scythians continued to push on conquering, for Herodotus goes on to say:

> After this they marched forward with the design of invading Egypt. When they had reached Palestine, however, Psammetichus the Egyptian king met them with gifts and prayers, and prevailed on them to advance no further.[73]

When Psammetichus became king of Egypt in 664 BCE, Assyria still held a tight grip over the country, which he was able to shake off over time, allowing him to reunite Egypt. Ashurbanipal could do little about the events transpiring in Egypt, since his borders were already buckling under pressure from systematic warfare with neighboring states. Thus, Ashurbanipal effectively pulled out of Egyptian affairs. Whether he removed Assyrian troops from Egypt is a matter of debate, for the Assyrian inscriptions are silent on this matter, other than some reliefs that depict the issues going on in Egypt.[74]

Assyrian troops would pull out of Philistia and the northern portions of what used to be the Northern Kingdom of Israel around 640 BCE. With Assyrian troops effectively gone from the region, Psammetichus moved into Philistia around 640 BCE,[75] while King Josiah of Judah pushed north to retrieve the remnants of Israel shortly after 630 BCE.[76] As for the Scythian invasion of Palestine, the year remains uncertain, but some suggest 626 BCE or shortly after.[77]

The reason for the Scythian invasion of Palestine seems to be due in part to the destabilization of the Assyrian Empire shortly after Ashurbanipal's death in 631 BCE. This led to the rise of his son Ashur-etil-ilani. Ashur-etil-ilani's reign would be very short and much undocumented. Ashur-etil-ilani would be deposed of in 627 BCE by a usurper named Sin-shumu-lishir, who reigned on the throne for a year or less.[78] With this transfer of power through what looks to be a *coup d'état*, the Assyrian Empire was fractured and open to foreign conquest.

Egypt at that time had been spreading its sphere of influence throughout Palestine, but how much land they controlled the further they pushed north remains unknown. It seems possible that when Sinsharishkun recaptured the throne in 626 BCE,[79] he sent messengers to the Scythians and Cimmerians to check the Egyptian advancement. But once the Scythians arrived on the scene they were paid off by the Pharaoh, as Herodotus mentions.[80] Another alternative as to why the Scythians may have pressed on into Palestine is that they felt the pressure of the Egyptian advancement northward. Remember, the Scythians had hegemony over the lands to the north of Palestine and felt the need to attack or at least check out their new neighbor. If so, then the Egyptians must have made an impression, for they paid off the Scythians with either a handsome gift or tribute.[81]

Herodotus' description shows that the Egyptians were weak in terms of military power but were rich in treasure, and therefore were able to bribe the Scythians from pillaging or conquest. In doing this, the Egyptians had exposed themselves, admitting their vulnerability, but at the same time showed their value. Treasure defeated the potential threat and allowed Egypt to carry on unopposed from the nomadic north to fight another day.

The amount of money given to the Scythians must have been great, but some decided to pillage "the temple of Celestial Aphrodite" at Ascalon, where "female sickness" overcame some few of the greedy. Those suffering from the curse would be deemed, "Enarees."[82]

Many do not accept the Scythian invasion of Palestine, finding the "female sickness" too similar to the story found in the book of I Samuel of how the Philistines got hemorrhoids in the same area that the Scythians would pass through later on. Tales can be intermingled over time. Another argument is that the Scythians were Assyrian mercenary troops assigned to certain posts to guard Assyria's interests and borders. This I agree with somewhat, as indicated earlier, for Assyria had pulled out of the region before the invasion took place, while others just outright reject the whole invasion.[83] However, I do think the Scythians really did invade Palestine, for "female sickness" is our clue.

Female sickness, according to Herodotus, created Enarees. The Enarees were women-like men who were soothsayers or prophets who received training from the goddess Aphrodite. These Enarees were not homosexual or transvestite, but rather transsexual, as implied by the Roman poet Ovid. Ovid tells us that these Enarees were young boys who had been castrated and says, "Ah me, that you, neither man nor woman, serve the lady; you who can't know the mutual delights of Venus! Whoever first cut off a boy's genitals, that one, who made the wound, should suffer it himself."[84] Ovid, in book 1 section 8 of the Amores, explains further concerning the process of male to female transsexual gender change. "She's a witch, mutters magical cantrips, can make rivers run uphill, knows the best aphrodisiacs – When to use herbal brews, or the whirring bullroarer, How to extract that stuff from a mare in heat."[85] The women are really men, and the urine that mares in heat produced allowed them to look more feminine, as Ovid explains. He tells the men to avoid this, and states, "Put no faith in herbals and potions, abjure the deadly stuff distilled by a mare in heat."[86] This deadly stuff is mare's urine. The urine from a pregnant mare is high in estrogen levels and helps males develop female sexual characteristics.[87]

Herodotus is partially right in his statement that the Scythians pillage the temple of Aphrodite at Ascalon. Nevertheless, the temple of Aphrodite Herodotus mentions most likely was the temple of the goddess

Atargatis,[88] where emasculation was practiced among the cult followers.[89]

The followers of Atargatis, particularly men, would dance to the music and work themselves into a frenzy of wild behavior. During the music and orgies, from among the onlookers of the frenzy, a young man taken up in the emotions of the frenzy would strip off his clothes, pick up a sword, and make a loud shout in the midst of the crowd, then castrate himself before the onlookers. Then he would run through the streets carrying his testicles in hand and from whatever house he threw his testicles in, he would receive women's garb to wear in order to join the temple priesthood of Atargatis.[90]

Notice that the priesthood of Atargatis is similar to the soothsayers and prophets of the Scythians. Both are castrated, both dress as women and have woman-like features. Thus, the few Scythians that pillaged the city or temple of Ascalon may not have pillaged the temple at all, but might have been caught up in the Atargatis cult. A few, if not all who were there, castrated themselves and brought the practice home, and Herodotus and many others would describe this later on. Therefore, the Scythian invasion of Palestine is proved by these two descriptions of the adoption of a local religious practice.

Besides the Scythian invasion of Palestine, Herodotus continues to explain that the Scythians went on to become masters of Media for the next twenty-eight years. That rule would end when Cyaxares invited the leaders to a banquet, rendered them defenseless by getting them drunk with wine, and massacred them. Afterward, the Medes regained their empire.[91]

Herodotus says that King Madyes reigned for those twenty-eight years, but I doubt it. If Madyes reigned for twenty-eight years, he would have had to start at the death of Dugdammi, which was around 640/39 BCE, and when you subtract twenty-eight years, we arrive at 612/11 BCE as the year of Madyes death. But if we take *The Fall of Nineveh Chronicle* into account, then Madyes would have to have died much earlier, because the first time we read of Cyaxares is in *The Fall of Nineveh Chronicle,* and according to its chronology, Cyaxares arrived on the scene in 614 BCE.[92] Thus, Madyes was dead and his reign over Asia after defeating Dugdammi did not last twenty-eight years as Herodotus says. Therefore, Cyaxares was free to go about his business in Asia unopposed as no Scythian threat seems near or far, and it could be argued that the Scythians, who did not oppose Cyaxares, joined his forces.

Whether or not the Scythians controlled the whole of Asia for twenty-eight years is true to some extent if you consider Dugdammi and add the reign of Madyes; then you have twenty-eight years and more. Now, this is not to say Herodotus is wrong, but from the time Nineveh fell in 612 BCE[93] to the Battle of the Eclipse or Halys, gives you twenty-eight years.[94] The notion of the Medes led by Cyaxares conquering a portion of Anatolia while bringing on the downfall of Urartu may in fact have been an invention of Herodotus.

Robert Rollinger's paper, *The Median "Empire", the End of Urartu and Cyrus' the Great Campaign in 547 B.C. (Nabonidus Chronicle II 16)*, makes a great argument that it was not the Medes who made their presence felt in Anatolia, but rather the Babylonians. This is shown in the inscription provided from *The Fall of Nineveh Chronicle* during the seventeenth year (609 BCE) of Nabopolassar's reign:

> The king of Akkad went to help his army and ... [...] he went up [to] Izalla and / the numerous cities in the mountains ... [...] he set fire to their [...] / At that time the army of [...] / [ma]rched / as far as the district of Urartu. / In the land ... [...] they plundered their [...].

The Babylonians in 608-607 BCE continued to attack Urartu and the surrounding area including eastern Anatolia, and according to the inscriptions, acted alone, without the help from the Medes, during the eighteenth year of Nabopolassar's reign. Overall, *The Fall of Nineveh Chronicle* supports a Babylonian domination of the north, including portions of eastern Anatolia. This does not mean that the Babylonians occupied or controlled the lands mentioned; rather they are the only ones named as having conducted military activities in the areas and having some influence over the regions for a time. At least until the arrival of Cyrus the Great in which the Nabonidus

Chronicle mentions that in 547 BCE Cyrus attacked and conquered the Kingdom of Urartu, leaving behind a garrison to watch over his newly acquired territory.

Therefore, I agree with Rollinger's conclusion concerning Herodotus and the Halys River in which he states, "Herodotus' image of the Median "Empire" has been modeled to a high degree on the Achaemenid Empire and the Halys border seems to be a much later invention."[95]

Beside the twenty-eight year domination by the Scythians, Herodotus goes on further to say:

> The dominion of the Scythians over Asia lasted eight-and-twenty years, during which time their insolence and oppression spread ruin on every side. For besides the regular tribute, they exacted from the several nations additional imposts, which they fixed at pleasure; and further, they scoured the country and plundered every one of whatever they could.[96]

This description is usual applied to Madyes. However, Herodotus may be attributing to Maydes acts described in the passage carried out by someone else, such as Dugdammi. Assyrian sources remain silent about Madyes and the troubles that came with him.

If Madyes did do the things that Herodotus suggests, whom did it affect? The civilizations of

Mesopotamia and Palestine, particularly Judah, seem to have escaped this ransacking. Egypt did pay a fee to the Scythians during what would have been the rule of Madyes. However, if we consider Dugdammi, mentioned in Assyrian sources, then we may have a case, for the Assyrians feared Dugdammi and it seems if anyone could get Assyria to pay tribute, Dugdammi would have been the person to do so. But even the Assyrians mention Dugdammi paying tribute to them. Therefore, I would suggest that the statement made by Herodotus is in fact much broader than he realized. In other words, if you consider the Scythians and Cimmerians from Esarhaddon to Ashurbanipal, you will find these nomadic peoples raiding and pillaging whoever they can whether it is Assyria, Lydia, or others in their vicinity. This is not to say Herodotus is wrong, but rather he is right in one sense and that is the Scythians and Cimmerians did in fact, regardless of the leader mentioned or not, before Madyes, pillage and raid. Madyes is not the pillager who is forcing tribute with ease as Herodotus tells.

As for the Scythian dominion that Herodotus speaks of, I do question whether the Scythians ruled as a single entity. It seems more plausible that they controlled Asia, not as a centralized united empire, but rather as a loose tribal community that goes about their own business, unless an outside element threatens their pastures and way of life. Consider the Assyrian inscriptions earlier in the book: the Assyrians name names, but none of chieftains seem to hold a firm grip on their own people, other than those tribes who are sympathetic to rebellion against Assyria. Once again, the only true Scythian king, according to Assyrian sources, was Dugdammi, but I am skeptical about Madyes kingship over the nomadic peoples.

During the Scythian-Cimmerian presence in Asia, most of the conquered or neighboring peoples would adopt the manners and customs of the Scythians and Cimmerians. The Assyrians, Babylonians, and others may have sent selected trainees to go to the Scythians to learn certain military skills, such as with bows and arrows, much desired by the regional powers, particularly Assyria, and then Babylonia.[97] Thus, Scythianization became the trend from Asia Minor to the Indus valley and from the Caucasus to the Persian Gulf for twenty-eight or more years. Once King Madyes died, Cyaxares hosted a banquet and invited the many Scythian chieftains, possibly in order to debate who should be king. However, the question remains, why did Cyaxares go on to massacre them?

Cyaxares invited Scythians of noble status and possibly many others, including those of non-Scythian birth. Every nomadic nation within the confines of the loosely held Scythian confederation was invited to dine and debate. As for the massacre, not everyone at the banquet was murdered.

I would suggest that the only people targeted were those that supported a continuation of an alliance with Assyria, or would protect Assyria in a time of crisis. This would be due to treaties and loyalty oaths that may have been undertaken when Madyes was alive and Assyria needed extra help in dealing with Dugdammi. The massacre that took place does not mean that Cyaxares hated the Scythian lords, but rather their continued policy of supporting the Assyrians. Remember, Cyaxares had no blood ties with the country, nor treaties or oaths to tie him to the Assyrians. Cyaxares most likely understood that a continued alliance with Assyria was dangerous due to its history of instability with neighboring countries.

There is an alternative to consider concerning the massacre: fratricide. This may be farfetched speculation, but Cyaxares actually may have been killing his brothers or cousins to acquire the throne of Madyes. Therefore, it is possible that the father of Cyaxares was Madyes. [98]

With a weakened Assyria stumbling around due to all the previous conflicts conducted by Ashurbanipal, the time was right for war. Once the personages of power who supported Assyria were removed, Cyaxares drove out the remainder who escaped execution. The forces of Cyaxares must have been in hot pursuit of those who did not yield to his rule. Cyaxares was in charge with no real threat to challenge him since both Madyes and Ashurbanipal were now dead. Cyaxares most likely thanked the gods that these "two birds" had been killed with one stone.

The Fall of Assyria

After King Ashurbanipal died, Assyria descended

into a slow agonizing chaos. One can argue that Assyria set itself back during the last years of Ashurbanipal's life, since much of that period remains silent. With ineffective kings sitting on the Assyrian throne taking turns just as quickly as they were seated, once prized holdings such as Babylonia slipped away from Assyrian control. This slip in power was a sign to the nations that bordered Assyria that the time to challenge it had come. To hesitate could be costly and bring on their demise. The first of these woes for Assyria started with Nabopolassar, king of Babylonia.

It has been said that Nabopolassar invaded Assyria to return the land to how it had been. This had largely to do with redrawing the borders between Babylonia and Assyria. Battles at the border had become so frequent that Assyria started receiving help from the Egyptians and Manneans, and because of the strength of arms showing up for the fight, Nabopolassar most likely went on the offensive hastily to protect his interests.[99]

In 616 BCE Nabopolassar marched his forces out of Babylonia and into Assyria. Once in Assyria, Nabopolassar followed the Euphrates River, where he encountered the Suhi and Hindanu tribes, who paid tribute to him. Three months later, the Assyrians prepared for battle in the city of Qablinu. Once Nabopolassar got word that the Assyrians were nearby, he quickly gathered his forces and advanced towards the city where he would do battle against the combined forces of the Assyrians and Manneans. Nabopolassar defeated them and took captive many of the Manneans who had aided the Assyrians in battle. The outcome of this battle would relieve pressure on the border of Babylon with Assyria, and at the same time secured the city of Uruk. Afterwards, Nabopolassar plundered and sacked the Mane, Sahiru, and Balihi, stealing their gods and goods, as well as the Hindanu, who were deported back to Babylon. On the journey back to Babylon, the combined forces of Egypt and Assyria made an unsuccessful strike at the forces of Nabopolassar near Qablinu. Later that year, Nabopolassar led his forces back into Assyria and did battle against them at Arraphu (modern day Kirkuk). Nabopolassar won the battle, pushed the remaining Assyrian forces back to the Zab River, and took many chariots and horses.

In 615 BCE Nabopolassar attempted to take the old Assyrian capital of Ashur, only to fail and retreat to the city of Takrit. Thus, he was now under siege himself by the Assyrian forces. The Assyrians, even though weak, were still able to field an army of considerable size. The battle for Takrit lasted ten days and in the end resulted in a very important victory for Nabopolassar. It is probable that during this time, the Umman-manda went down to Arraphu (modern Kirkuk) and took it. This would have meant that the Babylonians were never in control of Arraphu. If the Babylonians were in control of the city, you would expect them to have declared war on the Umman-manda for such an act. In addition, it suggests that the Babylonians would have been too weak to hold onto the city of Arraphu anyway, and may have over-extended themselves militarily, leading to their abandoning the city and region altogether.

In 614 BCE the Umman-manda attempted to sack Nineveh, but without results. They then turned their attention to the city of Tarbisu, which they captured. Soon after, the Umman-manda moved along the Tigris River until they came upon the ancient Assyrian capital of Ashur. The Umman-manda sacked and plundered Ashur and left nothing behind. Nabopolassar rushed his forces to the battle, but by the time they arrived, it was too late. Most importantly, Nabopolassar and Cyaxares became allies at the ruins of Ashur. To make this peace treaty and alliance legitimate, Nebuchadnezzar, son of Nabopolassar, married Amytis, daughter or granddaughter of Cyaxares.

Cyaxares and his Umman-mandan forces returned home for a short time, but in the process gained the relics of Ashur and the surrounding region. Nabopolassar and his Babylonians returned home displeased, demoralized by the destruction and treatment of Ashur. But on the positive side, Nabopolassar may have saved his kingdom from resembling Ashur through the marriage between Nebuchadnezzar and Amytis.[100] This may be mere romanticism than fact, but we should also consider that there is probably some truth behind this.[101]

In 613 BCE Nabopolassar faced few and sporadic rebellions along the Euphrates River. These rebellions by various smaller tribes were most likely in alliance with Assyria.[102] When Nabopolassar captured Anati on the Euphrates,[103] the king of Assyria marched his forces down the river towards Nabopolassar, who retreated and returned home. Some question why he returned home so rapidly, knowing that Assyria for the most part was just a shell of its former glory. The first answer to this question, may be the Scythians. Historians have speculated that either the Umman-manda switched sides for a brief time or that Scythians still loyal to Assyria came from the west. Actually, it may have been the Egyptians who aided the Assyrians at the Euphrates River and made their presence and size of force known to Nabopolassar.[104] This is probably why he retreated. The reason for Egypt's involvement is that under Necho II, they controlled and garrisoned the city of Carchemish. A cartouche and seal of Psammetichus I were found in a building at Carchemish, as well as one belonging to Necho II. Carchemish on the Euphrates River was under Egyptian control from 616 BCE to 605 BCE. It would have been easy for the Assyrians to ask the Egyptians for aid and to march along with them downriver to stop Nabopolassar.[105]

In 612 BCE Nabopolassar marched his forces into Assyria while Cyaxares and his Umman-manda forces came from the east to join him. Together they would combine their forces and besiege Nineveh. The siege lasted three months, until the walls finally tumbled. Once inside, the forces of the Babylonians and Umman-manda pillaged and looted the city, leaving only a broken shell with a dead king inside.

This was not the end for Assyria. The remaining survivors fled to Harran and a new king, Ashur-uballit, ascended the throne of Assyria. Afterward, Cyaxares returned home to Media, while Nabopolassar continued on, conquering Assyrian territory as far west as Nisibin. During this time, King Ashur-uballit partially reorganized what was left of Assyria, that being Harran. King Ashur-uballit sent a request to Egypt for aid, but at the same time retreated from the area. The Umman-manda were on their way to conquer Harran with the aid of Nabopolassar. King Ashur-uballit made his new home with the Egyptians at Carchemish. It was during this time that a throne change took place in Egypt, for Pharaoh Psammetichus died and his son Necho II had become the new Pharaoh. Pharaoh Necho II gave full support to Assyria by moving a large army to Carchemish. However, it was during this move that Necho II would stumble.[106]

King Josiah would also prove instrumental, even though it is not recorded on any Babylonian tablet. Josiah did in fact cause the Egyptians to stagnate in their attempt to aid Assyria. It seems that the seventeenth year of the reign of Nabopolassar is when Josiah king of Judah died. Scripture suggests that a large army tore rapidly out of Egypt to assist Assyria with re-taking the city of Harran. The Bible gives us a glimpse into the large army that was rushing to assist the King of Assyria. The scripture, found in II Chronicles 35:20-21, states:

> After all this, when Josiah had prepared the temple, Necho king of Egypt came up to fight against Charchemish by Euphrates: and Josiah went out against him.

> But he sent ambassadors to him saying, what have I to do with thee, thou king of Judah? I come not against thee this day, but against the house wherewith I have war: for God commanded me to make haste: forbear thee from meddling with God, who is with me, that he destroy thee not.

Necho knew that the best possible route to reach Harran was moving up the Mediterranean coast along the great trunk road, cutting across Josiah's newly re-conquered territory, formerly belonging to the Northern Kingdom of Israel, and then northward until reaching the city of Carchemish. From Carchemish, Necho would then go directly east until he reached Harran. Josiah, for the most part, disrupted the movement of Necho's forces. Necho says, "For God commanded me to make haste." Josiah's attack on Necho may have saved Harran from being re-taken by the Assyrians. Even though Josiah made Necho stumble before he got to Harran, retaliation from an Egyptian archer brought Josiah down. Josiah would lose his life supporting Babylonia and the Umman-manda unofficially.

Necho II would finally lead his army to Carchemish to help aid Ashur-uballit in his struggle against Babylonia and the Umman-manda. Nabopolassar came to the aid of Harran and defeated the forces brought across from Egypt.[107] The meager Assyrian army, along with the Egyptians, fled back to Carchemish for the time being, to reorganize and hope to fight another day. As for Ashur-uballit, Assyria's last king, his fate remains unknown. Ashur-uballit may have died attempting to retake Harran, but it is also possible that he died in 605 BCE when the mighty Babylonian forces crossed the Euphrates River and attacked the city of Carchemish, led by none other than the famed Nebuchadnezzar. Nebuchadnezzar would extinguish the last remnants of the Assyrian Empire, replacing it with another version known as Babylonia.[108]

Were the Scythians Involved with the Fall of Nineveh?

There has been much debate on whether or not the Scythians were involved with bringing down Assyria or supporting Assyria. The main argument against the Scythians coming to the aid of either side stems from the term Umman-manda mentioned in *The Fall of Nineveh Chronicle*. Some argue that the term Umman-manda can be applied to anyone and to suggest that it was just applied to Scythians or Cimmerians is false. I agree with this, for the term Umman-manda was applied to anyone from the north or considered uncivilized in the Mesopotamian mindset.

I find it important to address a few points of interest concerning Cyaxares, Medes, and the term Umman-manda, mentioned in *The Fall of Nineveh Chronicle*.

Before Herodotus jotted down the name Cyaxares, the first mention of Cyaxares is found in the chronicle dated to the twelfth year (614-613 BCE) of Nabopolassar's rule over Babylonia. The Chronicle mentions Cyaxares ruling over the Medes. In the fourteenth year (612-611 BCE) the term Umman-manda came to mean Medes. The rest of the chronicle continues to use the same names interchangeably.

While this is not in dispute, the term Mede is generic. The Assyrians and Babylonians called them Madaya, the Persians called them Mada, and the Greeks called them Medes. In other words, the term Mede is an extension of the region from which they come and that is Media. The region of Media is speculated to have extended from the Zagros Mountains in the west to the Caucasus in the north, while its southern neighbor was Ellipi. How far Media extended to the east remains in dispute.[109] Therefore, the amount of territory under Median control sounds a bit exaggerated if we believe that it reached all the way to India, and if it is true that they did control a vast amount of land, there is no way all of the people under their sphere of influence were Medes.

Tiglath-pileser invaded the region of Media in 737 and 736 BCE. In both invasions, Tiglath-pileser subdued and deported many Medes westward into Assyria. Tiglath-pileser is said to have deported 65,000 Medes on one occasion. Sargon II also invaded the area and deported Medes from the region. In both deportations, resettlement involved placing new nations into the region that had been cleared of the recent dwellers. These new occupants of Media, like the Israelites, from the Northern Kingdom of Israel, II Kings 17:6,[110] would become the new owners of the land, like the many others placed alongside them.

If we take into account that newly conquered nations like Israel, among the many others who were uprooted from their original homeland and resettled into Median lands, the occupiers of this region are no more Median then a Median is an Israelite or even an Aramean. Therefore, for the Babylonians to call the Umman-manda "Medes" is correct, but in a different context. In other words, those deported to Media became the new Medes, and to the Babylonians the region from which the Umman-manda is coming from is from Media. Thus, the term Mede is used to describe the region with which the Umman-manda are associated. Therefore, Cyaxares is leading a mixed multitude including Scythians, Cimmerians, and Medes, as well as many other ethnic groups under the banner of the region they came from, which is Media.

Endnotes: Chapter Four

[1] Mark William Chavalas, *The Ancient Near East: Historical Sources in Translation*. (Malden, MA: Blackwell, 2006), 358/ Saggs, 109.

[2] M. Cogan & H. Tadmor, *Gyges and Ashurbanipal: a study in literary transmission*", in: Orientalia 46 (1977), 68.

[3] Dandamaev, Lukonin, Kohl, and Dadson, 53.

[4] Cogan & Tadmor, *Gyges and Ashurbanipal: a study in literary transmission* 81-82.

[5] Hans Jürgen Tertel, *Text and Transmission: An Empirical Model for the Literary development of Old Testament Narratives,* (Germany: Walter De Gruyter Inc, 1994), 147.

[6] Kristensen, 100.

[7] Ibid.

[8] Charles Brian Rose, G. Darbyshire, and Keith DeVries, *The New Chronology of Iron Age Gordion* (Philadelphia: University of Pennsylvania Museum of Archaeology and Anthropology, 2012), 53.

[9] Kristensen, 100.

[10] Erich Ebeling, and Bruno Meissner. *Reallexikon Der Assyriologie Und Vorderasiatischen Archaologie* . (Berlin: Walter De Gruyter, 1987), 621.

[11] Martti Nissinen, Robert Kriech Ritner, C. L. Seow, and Peter Machinist. *Prophets and prophecy in the ancient Near East*, (Atlanta, GA: Society of Biblical Literature, 2003), 144-145.

[12] Mary Boyce, *A history of Zoroastrianism*, (Leiden: E.J. Brill, 1982), 11.

[13] Donald B. Redford, *Egypt, Canaan, and Israel in Ancient Times,* (Princeton, New Jersey: Princeton University Press, 1993), 406.

[14] Capt, 126

[15] http://www.kent.net/DisplacedDynasties/NebuchadnezzarChapter3.htm

[16] Capt, 126.

[17] Gocha R. Tsetskhladze, *North Pontic Archaeology: Recent Discoveries and Studies,* (Leiden: Brill, 2001), 39.

[18] Drews, 95.

[19] Simo Parpola, *Letters from Assyrian scholars to the kings Esarhaddon and Assurbanipal . Repr. Ed*, (Winona Lake, Ind.: Eisenbrauns, 2007), 220.

[20] Saggs, 109-117.

[21] Strabo 1.3.21.

[22] Kristensen, 100.

[23] Gocha R. Tsetskhladze, *North Pontic Archaeology: Recent Discoveries and Studies*, 39.
[24] Georg Morgenstierne, Jacques Duchesne-Guillemin, *Monumentum Georg Morgenstierne, Issue 21 Volumes 21-22 of Acta Iranica*, (Leiden: E.J. Brill, 1981), 117.
[25] Simo Parpola, C. H. W. Johns, and Knut Leonard Tallqvist. *Neo-Assyrian toponyms*, (Kevelaer: Butzon & Bercker, 1970), 138.
[26] Ivantchik, 99-100, 278-281.
[27] J.Maxwell Miller and John H. Hayes, *A History of Ancient Israel and Judah*, (Philadelphia: Westminster Press, 1986), 38.
[28] Kristensen, 100.
[29] Georg Morgenstierne, Jacques Duchesne-Guillemin, *Monumentum Georg Morgenstierne, Issue 21 Volumes 21-22 of Acta Iranica*, 117.
[30] Gocha Tsetskhladze, *Ancient West & East, Volume 3, Issue 2*, (Leiden: Brill, 2004), 234, note 40.
[31] A. H. Sayce, *The Early History of the Hebrews*, (London: Rivingtons, 1897), 26.
[32] Mackenzie, Donald A. *Myths of Babylonia and Assyria*, (London: Gersham Publishing Company Limited , 2004), 222.
[33] Chavalas, 37.
[34] Glassner, and Foster, 221.
[35] David Stephen Vanderhooft, *The Neo-Babylonian Empire and Babylon in the latter Prophets*, (Atlanta, Ga.: Scholars Press, 1999), 21.
[36] A. Leo Oppenheim, *Ancient Mesopotamia: Portrait of a Dead Civilization*, (Chicago & London: The University of Chicago Press, 1964), 397.
[37] Ivantchik, 99-100.
[38] Ibid, 281.
[39] Chavalas, 156.
[40] J.Maxwell Miller and John H. Hayes, *A History of Ancient Israel and Judah*, 38.
[41] King James Bible.
[42] Robert H. Pfeiffer and Robert Francis Harper. *State Letters of Assyria; A Transliteration and Translation of 355 Official Assyrian Letters Dating from the Sargonid Period (722-625 B.C.)*. New Haven, Conn: American oriental society, 1935), 219.
[43] Ibid, 220.
[44] Ivantchik, 268-269.

[45] Halet Çambel and John David Hawkins, *Corpus of Hieroglyphic Luwian Inscriptions: Inscriptions of the Iron Age*, (Berlin: Walter de Gruyter, 2000), 428.
[46] Ivantchik, 271-272.
[47] Ibid, 273.
[48] Ibid, 274.
[49] Patricia Turner and Charles Russell Coulter, *Dictionary of Ancient Deities*, (New York: Oxford University Press, 2001), 185.
[50] Herodotus, *The Histories* 1.216, 4. 106.
[51] Timothy Kandler Beal, *Religion and its Monsters*, (New York: Routledge, 2002), 17-19.
[52] Ivantchik, 271-272.
[53] Strabo, *The Geography*, 1.3.21
[54] Ivantchik, 274.
[55] Ibid., 271-272.
[56] Georg Morgenstierne, Jacques Duchesne-Guillemin, *Monumentum Georg Morgenstierne, Issue 21 Volumes 21-22 of Acta Iranica*, 117.
[57] Simo Parpola, *Letters from Assyrian scholars to the kings Esarhaddon and Assurbanipal . Repr. Ed*, 220.
[58] Will Slatyer, *Life/Death Rhythms of Ancient Empires – Climatic Cycles Influence Rule of Dynasties* (Singapore: Trafford On Demand Pub, 2012), 42-43.
[59] Gwendolyn Leick, *Historical dictionary of Mesopotamia*, (Lanham, MD: Scarecrow Press, 2003), 64.
[60] Strabo, *The Geography*, 1.3.21
[61] Thomas R. Kämmerer, *Studien zu Ritual und sozialgeschichte im Alten Orient = Studies on ritual and society in the ancient Near East : Tartuer Symposien, 1998-2004*, (Berlin: Walter De Gruyter, 2007), 167.
[62] Ivantchik, 115.
[63] Roux, 332-333.
[64] Strabo, *The Geography*, 1.3.21
[65] Ivantchik, 274.
[66] Gocha R. Tsestkhladze, *Ancient Greeks West and East: edited by Gocha R. Tsetskhladze,* (Leiden: Brill, 1999), 508.
[67] Arrian, Arrianus, Flavius *Anabasis of Alexander, Books 5-7. Indica. / with an Engl. transl. by P.A. Brunt.- Revised text and translation with new introd., notes and appendices ed,(*Cambridge, Mass: Harvard University, 1983), 319.
[68] Herodotus, *The Histories* 1.103
[69] Tsestkhladze, 509.

[70] Karen Radner, "Knowledge and Power - The royal family: queen, crown prince, eunuchs and others." Knowledge and Power - Knowledge and Power in the Neo-Assyrian Empire. http://knp.prs.heacademy.ac.uk/essentials/royalfamily/ (accessed April 26, 2011).
[71] Herodotus, *The Histories* 1.103
[72] Herodotus, *The Histories* 1.104
[73] Ibid, 1.105
[74] Robert Morkot, *Historical Dictionary of Ancient Egyptian Warfare*, (Lanham, Md.: Scarecrow Press, 2003), 35, 37.
[75] Ephraim Stern, *Archaeology of the land of the Bible the Assyrian, Babylonian, and Persian periods, 732-332 BCE*, (New York: Doubleday, 2001), 107.
[76] Joseph Blenkinsopp, *A History of prophecy in Israel*, (Philadelphia: Westminster Press, 1996), 140.
[77] Askold Ivantchik, *The Scythian 'Rule Over Asia': the Classical Tradition and the Historical Reality: Ancient Greeks West and East. Ed. Gocha R. Tsetskhladze. Mnemosyne Supplement 196*, (Boston: Brill, 1999), 516-517.
[78] Nadav Na'aman, *Chronology and History in the Late Assyrian Empire 631-619 BC*, (Zeitschrift für Assyriologie, 81, 1991), 243-267.
[79] Nadav Na'aman, *Chronology and History in the Late Assyrian Empire 631-619 BC,* 243-267.
[80] Herodotus, *The Histories* 1.105.
[81] Kristensen, 100.
[81] Ibid, 100.
[82] Herodotus, *The Histories* 1.105
[83] Redford, 440.
[84] Ovid, *The Amores*, 2.3.
[85] Ibid. 1.8.
[86] Ovid, *On Facial Treatment for Ladies*, 36-37.
[87] Walter O. Bockting, and Eli Coleman, *Gender Dysphoria: Interdisciplinary Approaches in Clinical Management*, (New York: Hayworth Press, 1993), 46.
[88] Egerton Sykes, and Alan Kendall, *Who's Who in Non-Classical Mythology*, (London: Routledge, 2002), 20.
[89] K. van der Toorn, Bob Becking, and Pieter Willem van der Horst, *Dictionary of Deities and Demons in the Bible DDD*, (Leiden: Brill, 1999), 115.
[90] Lucian, Herbert Augustus Strong, and John Garstang. *The Syrian Goddess Being a Translation of Lucian's De Dea Syria, with a Life of*

Lucian by Herbert A. Strong. Edited with Notes and an Introd. by John Garstang, (London: Constable, 1913), 59.

[91] Herodotus, *The Histories,* 1.106.
[92] Glassner, and Foster, 219-225.
[93] Ibid. 223.
[94] Herodotus, *The Histories,* 1.74.
[95] Robert Rollinger, "The Median 'Empire', the End of Urartu and Cyrus the Great's Campaign in 547 BC: (Nabonidus Chronicle II 16)." Ancient West & East 7 (2008): 51-65. http://poj.peeters-leuven.be/content.php?url=article&id=2033252 (accessed May 20, 2011).
[96] Herodotus, *The Histories,* 1.106.
[97] Dandamaev, Lukonin, Kohl, and Dadson, 226.
[98] Herodotus, *The Histories,* 1.106.
[99] Saggs, 118-120.
[100] A.T. Olmstead, History of Assyria, (Chicago: The University of Chicago Press, 1951), 634-637.
[101] Maria Brosius, *Women in Ancient Persia, 559-331 B.C.* (Oxford: Clarendon, 1998), 43.
[102] Saggs, 119.
[103] Jean-Jacques Glassner, and Benjamin R. Foster, *Mesopotamian Chronicles,* 221.
[104] Saggs, 119.
[105] Edward Lipinski, *On the Skirts of Canaan in the Iron Age: Historical and Topographical Researches*, (Leuven: Uitgeverij Peeters en Departement Oosterse Studies, 2006), 157.
[106] Saggs, 120.
[107] Olmstead, 638-639.
[108] Saggs, 121.
[109] M. Dandamayev and I. Medvedskaya. "Media" Encyclopædia Iranica, Online Edition, January 6, 2006, available at http://www.iranica.com/articles/media.
[110] Ebeling and Meissner, 621.

5

Conclusion

The history of the Scythian and Cimmerian peoples during the Neo-Assyrian Empire demonstrates a new type of warrior to appear on the horizon of history and make his mark, starting with the Battle on Mt. Uaush in 714 BCE.

The Assyrians seem to have been the builders of this nomadic people during the reign of Sargon II. However, they may have been as they were long before the Assyrians ever took notice of them and utilized them in the Assyrian military apparatus. But I find this difficult to accept and must say that the Cimmerians and Scythians were indeed a byproduct of the Assyrian war machine. But not entirely, for their weapons and armor show a Near Eastern influence, suggesting that they were from the Near East, but from where is another matter. In addition, their tactics seem to have been useless when fighting the Assyrians. When some of the nomadic chieftains rose up in rebellion against their Assyrian masters, we do not read of any description of swarming or feinting, and only later were they able to find a system that worked best. This does not mean that these tactics were not already in use, but I would argue that only later were such tactics demonstrated as a group.

The Assyrians, you could say, created a monster, a nomadic monster, which started with the various Scythian and Cimmerian chieftains who rebelled, but one in particular really showed the Assyrians what they did create and his name is Dugdammi. So scared was Ashurbanipal that Dugdammi was referred to as "King of the World," which says a lot about the power of these nomads and the weakening of Assyria. It took another Scythian to take down Dugdammi. This may be an indication that the tactics and organization were equal or superior to that of the Assyrians. However, it may show the opposite and suggest that the Assyrians were too fractured militarily and socially to take on the new challenger for fear of losing their empire.

With Ashurbanipal's death, the Assyrian Empire began to crumble and cave in to internal conflict; thus allowing outside elements to venture in, starting with the Babylonians and afterwards the Umman-manda, led by Cyaxares.

Assyria would soon crumble after these events and the Scythians and Cimmerians were still in the region, particularly Media, during the reign of Cyaxares. I would argue against Herodotus' notion of the events between Cyaxares and the Scythians in a chronological view.

What the Scythians and Cimmerians brought to history is still somewhat of a mystery. Herodotus, Strabo, and many other ancient Historians spoke of these peoples, but were limited to some degree and in some cases added a sense of bias against them or tried to compare them with their own cultures. The Scythian and Cimmerian peoples were the exact opposite of what some desired them to be or thought. But without their comments, we would still be in the dark. Thankfully we have the Assyrian inscriptions that go into great detail. By taking those inscriptions along with those who wrote about them outside of Assyria, we begin to see a somewhat clear but still fuzzy picture of these nomadic peoples.

These people were nomadic and wild, but displayed an ability to fight like no other in the Near East. Bow and arrow, lance and armor, horse underneath, they were indeed the creators of the first cavalry knight long before medieval knights of Europe. Their combat was tactical and superior for many centuries to come, and even today, many still use similar tactics, whether guerrilla fighters or U.S. Special Operations using tactically clandestine methods, even when engaged on the battlefield.

The Scythians and Cimmerians were masters of the horse and bow and formed a mobile army that could travel without hindrance, unlike the established civilizations in Mesopotamia at the time, and they would continue as masters of Asia and parts of Europe, north of the Black Sea, for many centuries to come.

They are legends and timeless, and I hope more will find them interesting enough to continue researching them, for they are history's first true nomadic warriors, able to engage and defeat the strongest armies, and live in places that seem untouchable, like themselves.

Appendix I

Arms and Armor

The arms and armor of the Cimmerians and Scythians are indeed unique. The one thing we shall notice is the evolution of their arms and armor over time. This was necessary due to the forces they faced and the harsh terrain they lived on, which caused them to change and adapt to their enemy quickly. They studied what best worked for them in peacetime and implemented it during wartime to give the opponent the maximum effect.

Before we start to examine the arms and armor of the Cimmerians and Scythians, it is necessary to lump them together as one entity. The reason is that these two groups are difficult to tell apart due to their similar lifestyle. Only by name do we get an idea of who they are, but as you will read, even this can be intricate. Therefore, we must examine the early period first and work our way through history, noticing the ever-changing styles of arms and armor of these nomadic equestrians before we go into the early accounts told by those who faced or observed them.

Body Armor

The description you are about to read may sound as if body armor had an appearance somewhat like that of the Medieval knights of Europe. The Greek historian, Herodotus, describes in detail how these nomadic equestrians looked in military apparel:

> In their dress and mode of living the Massagetae resemble the Scythians. They fight both on horseback and on foot, neither method is strange to them: they use bows and lances, but their favorite weapon is the battle-axe. Their arms are all either of gold or brass. For their spear points, and arrow-heads, and for their battle-axes, they make use of brass; for head-gear, belts, and girdles, of gold. So too with the caparison of their horses, they give them breastplates of brass, but employ gold about the reins, the bit, and the cheek-plates. They use neither iron nor silver, having none in their country; but they have brass and gold in abundance.[1]

Another description of Scythian body armor comes from the historian Justin, in which he states, "Their armor, and that of their horses, is formed of plates, lapping over one another like the feathers of a bird, and covers both man and horse entirely."[2] The two descriptions show a well-armored horse and rider. However, this raises a question: who influenced these nomads to cover their mounts and themselves in armor? The answer may point to none other than Mesopotamians.

The Assyrians may have influenced the Cimmerians and Scythians to use body armor and develop it further. The historian and archaeologist Tadeusz Sulimirski makes note of this and mentions that the Scythian armored cavalry was a mirror image of the Assyrian cavalry.[3] This tells us the Scythians and Cimmerians are close to the Assyrians in both political and military relations, as you will read about later.

The Assyrians wore what is called lamellar armor. Assyrian armor was composed of leather, sewn or glued together; next, they would attach iron or bronze plates to the hardened leather. Each individual plate was joined to the next with no overlapping and held in place with either stitching or glue. The total weight of the Assyrian corselet is roughly thirty pounds, making the corselet light and flexible to maneuver in.[4]

The armor corselet of the Scythians and Cimmerians is somewhat similar. Scythians and Cimmerians were archers first, but not all were light archers. The type of armor they wore would have been of a lighter, more flexible material of hardened leather or hide,[5] sometimes overlapped with iron or bronze scales. The metal scales used to overlap the leather or hardened hide had to be cut from a sheet of metal with special tools. Once cut, the individual pieces were attached to the soft leather using leather thongs or animal tendons. Each scale was positioned sideways to the next, overlapping about one-third or one-half of the next scale. This would protect the stitching so as not to expose it to hand or projectile weaponry. Once the corselet was finished, it had the look of fish scales.

The body armor varied, for not every Scythian or Cimmerian wore full body armor from front to back. Some variations are from the neck down to the upper breast, while others had a fully armored front but not the back. Short-sleeved corselets are common and only a few long-sleeved corselets have been found. Some used extra scaled body armor that is in smaller pieces. Smaller armor was placed on the upper back, over the shoulders and covering the sides of the breast/chest. Smaller (plates/scaled pieces) like the ones used for the shoulders were utilized to protect the elbows of the rider as well.[6] These smaller plates allowed for maximum flexibility for a rider to function properly on the field of battle with little hindrance to movement.

Overall, the design of the Scythian corselet is made to take a pounding. With overlapping scales protecting the next scale as well as protecting the stitching underneath, it would take a well-sustained volley of arrows for even one arrow to find a space just wide enough to penetrate and injure or kill a man.

Shin armor, like the upper body armor, is also made of leather covered with metal scales or plates. The Scythians would replace this type of armor in favor of greaves, like the ones the Greeks wore, which are also made of metal and were solid rather than scaled. However, these solid metal greaves may have been limited to heavy cavalry.[7] Although many images depict the Scythians in light war attire, only a few depict them in full body armor. The Scythians would also decorate these solid metal greaves with images of the face of the Gorgon on the knees, while the sides of the greaves depicted snakes slithering down.[8] These images, like many in the ancient world, whether on a shield, breastplate, or greaves, were designed to intimidate the enemy. The face of the Gorgon used by the Scythians is indeed to inspire fear, for the Gorgon represents sudden death. The Scythians had a weapon that could inflict sudden death: snake venom, which is an issue we will discuss shortly.[9]

Much of the artwork that depicts the Scythians shows them in light armor versus the heavy armor mentioned earlier. Many Scythians and Cimmerians who wore heavy armor may have been nobility. Herodotus mentions a group known as the Royal Scythians who lived north of the Black Sea. Herodotus describes them as being "the largest and bravest of the Scythian tribes, which looks upon all the other tribes in the light of slaves." These other nomadic tribes are commoners or common Scythians who hold no title of nobility. Herodotus describes them as being "separated" by the Gerrhus River from the Royal Scythians and says, "This river on its passage towards the sea divides the country of the Nomadic from that of the

Royal Scyths."[10] Herodotus' description of the nomadic and royal Scythians suggests that there were far more horse archers than heavy cavalry, based on social class. An example of social class can be observed in the Battle of Carrhae between Rome and Parthia in 53 BCE. Plutarch, a Roman historian, mentions that horse archers do not engage the Roman forces, but the heavy Parthian cavalry would lance through the Roman lines,[11] whereas Herodotus makes the claim that earlier Massagetae horsemen are well-armored. This is not to say they were not, but we should not assume that all of the Scythian sub-tribes were armor clad.

Figure 5 Armored Scythian Cavalryman[12]

Figure 6 Parthian Horse Archers[13]

Helmet

The helmets or headgear worn by the Scythians and Cimmerians seem to differ, according to the various art pieces that depict them. Many art pieces show the Scythians wearing the traditional soft hood or pointed cap,[14] while other images show them wearing the bronze kuban style helmet, named after the Kuban River in the North Caucasus region from which they were discovered.[15] Those who wore the bronze helmet were most likely chieftains, lesser nobility, and perhaps men of wealth.[16]

However, we must also consider that some Scythian and Cimmerian tribes wore armored helmets as a group. An example of this would be from the battle of Gaugamela in 331 BCE between Alexander the Great of Macedonia and Darius III of Persia. The historian Arrian mentions that at Gaugamela, "the Scythians themselves and their horses were protected by armor."[17] Arrian's description of the Scythians at Gaugamela provides the possibility that some Scythian tribal elements were fully armored from head to toe. It is possible that Scythians who were at Gaugamela were wealthy enough to buy the armor alongside those who inherited their armor, e.g., nobility.

As for the origins of the Scythian helmet, they remain disputed, but it seems to have originated in the Near East. Some historians suggest the design and style of the early Scythian Kuban helmet is a prototype influenced by China,[18] while others argue that the design of the helmet originated in the regions of either the Caucasus or Central Asia.[19] At first some argued a Near Eastern origin was not possible since no known prototype had been discovered. The helmet these nomads wore seems to have been influenced by the Elamites, who wore a similar style helmet during their Middle period. The connection to the Elamite variation is shown by a similar cutout of the eyebrows on the Kuban helmet and the rib that runs along the rim of the eyebrow curves, almost like the shape of a bow. In other words, the Kuban helmet is an open-faced helmet like that of the Elamites. It is said to be the earliest known version of this type or likeness that the Scythians wore. The helmet the Elamites wore seems influenced by the conical helmet of the Scythians.[20]

The Assyrian conical helmet depicted is cone shaped and may have influenced the Scythians, who were famous for wearing a soft, pointed, conical hood.[21] Additionally, some Scythians and Cimmerians donned the bronze conical helmet at the same time, which suggests an adoption of the Assyrian helmet through direct influence.[22]

The helmet in question is likely a Chinese and Near Eastern blend. Therefore, it comes down to a matter of whom these nomads associated themselves with in regards to the China or Near East origin debate and the type of warfare for which the helmet is best suited. Assyria is the first to mention them in inscriptions due to the Cimmerians and Scythians staying in close contact with them. Thus, if any culture had any real influence as to what the Cimmerians and Scythians would wear, it would have been the Assyrians and their neighbors. Most of the Scythian arms and armor exhibit a Near Eastern influence.

Figure 7 Soft Pointed Caps

23

Figure 8 Assyrian wearing conical helmet[24]

Weapons

The Cimmerians and Scythians used a variety of offensive weapons, including the axe, spear, javelin, sword, dagger, and their famous composite bow. Let us first examine the battle-axe and work our way through the weaponry of these nomads.

Axe

According to Herodotus, the Scythians carried a battle-axe, or sagaris. He mentions its use among the Massagetae Scythians.[25] Xenophon mentions the use of the sagaris among the Amazons.[26] The sagaris has an odd shape and is lightweight. Most axes are in line with the handle, but the sagaris looks more like an ice pick, making it a very lethal and practical side weapon for combat.[27] Notice Figure 5 on the next page, which shows a Scythian with a sagaris in hand that has a small axe blade and spiked butt. The interesting shape of the sagaris is similar to the Assyrian battle-axe, for many of the battle-axes utilized by the Scythians are of Assyrian design or style.[28]

Figure 9 Scythian with sagaris in right hand

Lance

The Scythians also used lances in combat. The length of the lance is 3 meters long (9.84 Feet).[30] In the tomb of Anthesterius located at Kerch, Ukraine, a fresco depicts a Scythian yurt with a lance measuring 15 to 20 feet long leaning against the yurt. The same fresco depicts a Scythian heavy cavalryman in combat carrying a lance of the same length.[31] Herodotus mentions the Massagetae Scythians using the lance against the Persian forces led by Cyrus the Great:

> First, the two armies stood apart and shot their arrows at each other; then, when their quivers were empty, they closed and fought hand-to-hand with lances and daggers.

Cyrus died in battle against the Massagetae, as mentioned by Herodotus.[32] According to Babylonian sources, the event of his death took place around 530 BCE.[33] Herodotus' description of the battle is vague, but what is intriguing is the mention of the lance used by the Massagetae. Herodotus goes on further to say "they use bows and lances."[34] Earlier, we discussed the armor the Scythians and Cimmerians wore. In regard to the lance and armor mentioned earlier, the first thing that comes to mind is a medieval knight. The description of the Massagetae by Herodotus tells us that these heavy cavalrymen not only carried the lance but the bow as well.

However, one must be careful not to lump one tribal element of Scythians in with another.

The Massagetae may have worn full armor and may have had other units that carried the lance, making them look knightly. On the other hand, many Scythians and Cimmerians were neither heavily armored nor did they carry a lance; they were primarily horse archers in light war attire. This calls Herodotus' description into question concerning an entire tribe of Scythians being heavily armored and cavalry-based. But if Herodotus were right in his description, this would suggest the Massagetae were a tribe utilizing heavy cavalry to combat the heavy infantry used by their neighbors, such as Persia.[35] On the other hand, Herodotus could be wrong in his account and the Massagetae that you read about might have been the nobility of the tribe.

Figure 10 Parthian horsemen carrying a lance or javelin

Javelin

Little is mentioned about the use of the javelin by the Scythians; however, the Scythians seem to have mastered its use, according to a Roman poet by the name of Virgil, who described "Scythians, expert in the dart and bow."[37] Once the Scythians had used their entire inventory in their quiver, the javelin became the secondary projectile weapon of choice.[38] Both spears and javelins were used rarely, for Scythians preferred to fight from afar.[39] This would make sense, for to use a spear or javelin from horseback requires close combat, risking both rider and horse if the enemy on foot has a similar weapon or if archers are among their ranks.

Javelins, spears, and darts, whichever you prefer to call them, were of various lengths. One javelin discovered at Chertomlyk, Ukraine, was 7 feet long.[40] Other javelins vary from about 1.7 meters (5.58 feet) to 1.8 meters (5.91 feet) in length, making the one discovered at Chertomlyk very long.[41]

The metal used to create the spearhead of the javelin was made of copper, bronze, or iron.[42] The length and shape also determined the role of the projectile. The length of the longer spearheads is around 71 centimeters or 27.9 inches in length[43] and were designed to penetrate armor. Shorter spearheads measuring around 30 cm or 11.8 inches are usually in the shape of a pyramid and designed to lodge in the flesh of the enemy, thus making it harder to pull out.[44] An example would be the Roman javelin known as the "pilum," which was designed to lodge in the flesh or shield of the enemy, either causing excruciating pain or frustrating attempts to free the shield, rendering it useless and causing it to be tossed aside by the combatant. Nevertheless, the Scythian javelin, unlike the Roman pilum, did not break or bend upon impact.[45]

Sword

Did the Scythian warrior carry a sword? Most artwork depicting the Scythians shows an absence of the sword, but not entirely. Most people think of a sword as being rather long and threatening, like in the movies. The images people see show what the Scythians seem to revere most, and that is the bow. The sword seems almost absent from portrayals. The sword the Scythians carried was rather short, giving the illusion that it is only a dagger. This is partially right and wrong. Scythians did carry a sword, but the image was rare in stone reliefs or metal artwork, making the sword seem nonexistent at times. It is interesting to note that even though the sword rarely makes an appearance in the images depicting them, the Scythians actually worshipped the sword. Herodotus gives a fine description of sword worship, saying:

> Such are the victims offered to the other gods, and such is the mode in which they are sacrificed; but the rites paid to Mars are different. In every district, at the seat of

government, there stands a temple of this god, whereof the following is a description. It is a pile of brushwood, made of a vast quantity of fagots, in length and breadth three furlongs; in height somewhat less, having a square platform upon the top, three sides of which are precipitous, while the fourth slopes so that men may walk up it. Each year a hundred and fifty wagon-loads of brushwood are added to the pile, which sinks continually by reason of the rains. An antique iron sword is planted on the top of every such mound, and serves as the image of Ares: yearly sacrifices of cattle and of horses are made to it, and more victims are offered thus than to all the rest of their gods.

Herodotus mentions in the passage that the Scythians worshipped Mars, the god of war. This is unlikely. Rather Herodotus is trying to connect the Greeks to the Scythians through religious and ethnic means, such as when he says Hercules was the father of the Scythians.[46] Nevertheless, when dealing with the sword and god, the rhetoric writer Lucian gives a different impression than Herodotus, "because wind is the source of life, and sword is that which causes to die."[47] Whether or not the Scythians revered the sword as the Greek god of war or even death, they treated the sword second best in combat. In other words, the sword was a secondary weapon, not used until all projectiles were exhausted in battle. However, even if they ran out of every arrow, javelin, or spear, the Scythians were still reluctant to fight up close and personal unless they had no choice.

The sword they carried was rather short when compared to other sword lengths and in the words of Ellis H. Minns, "Hardly any of them are worthy to be called swords."[48] The reason for Minns' statement is that many of the found swords border between a sword and a dagger, which leaves us with the akinakes. The sword the Scythians and perhaps the Cimmerians carried is an akinakes, which is mistaken for a "scimitar." This is misleading, for the akinakes is short and straight and the scimitar is curved.[49]

The akinakes also has a spiritual and regal side to it. The Persian King Xerxes, before he crossed over the Hellespontos, sacrificed his own akinakes by tossing it into the straits. Xerxes also gave a gold akinakes as a gift to the people of Abdera as he came back from Greece.[50] Xenophon mentions that Cyrus the younger gave an akinakes to Syennesis, king of Tarsos[51] and also gave one to his servant, Artapatas.[52] Overall, the akinakes was revered as a spiritual weapon that was symbolic of divine justice, a physical symbol of authority among the Persians and Scythians.

The akinakes were attached to the girdle by a patch, in which a cord is passed through a hole, while the bottom part of the scabbard is fixed to the thigh with cord as well. The length of the blade varies; most common lengths around the 7th century BCE seem to be roughly 40-50 cm (15.7 to 19.6 inches). The grip of the sword was 12-14 cm (4.7 to 5.5 inches). In total, the Scythian/Cimmerian sword is roughly 20.4 inches to 25.1 inches in length, making it close to two feet. In addition, the sword becomes somewhat longer later on, reaching a length between 60-80 cm (23.6 inches to 31.5 inches in length.

Another interesting aspect about these archaic blades is the scabbards that held them. Many of the scabbards are a combination of wood and gold. The wood has long since rotted away, but the gold is intact. The decorations engraved upon the gold suggest a Neo-Assyrian or Persian influence. Some decorations, but not all, feature lions with fish wings and various other monsters from Mesopotamian mythology. However, as time passes, many of the scabbards are still the same but the images change. Scythians once influenced by Mesopotamian culture are later influenced by the Greek culture. The Scythian scabbard that once displayed images of Mesopotamian monsters and figures now displays individual combat scenes on horse or on foot in the Greek style.[53]

Figure 11 Mithra holding an Akinakes[54]

Figure 12 Darius the Great holding an
Akinakes in left hand

Figure 13 Cimmerians

The Bow and Arrow

The Scythian and Cimmerian bow is unique and revered throughout the ancient world by kings, historians, and a philosopher. King Esarhaddon of Assyria had a Cimmerian bow, the Babylonian armies of Nebuchadnezzar II and Nabonidus were equipped with their bows and arrows, and even Hercules' Greek portrait displays him armed with a Scythian bow.[57] The Greek philosopher. Plato, said, "The customs of the Scythians proves our error; for they not only hold the bow from them with the left hand and draw the arrow to them with their right, but use either hand for both purposes."[58] Plato's description shows that the Scythians were indeed expert archers. Like the Japanese Samurai who were one with the sword, the same can be said about the Scythians being one with the bow.

The weapon was indeed a favorite among the later Mesopotamian empires. What made this weapon special is quite interesting. The bow used by these nomads does not look like anything special when viewed, but back then it was a new, threatening, and revolutionary weapon. It would slowly replace the angular bow used by the Assyrians and much of the Near East. When Assyria fell, the Cimmerian and Scythian bow was the bow of choice among civilizations. Its use spread from the Iranian plateau, made its way westward through Greece, and finally reached the shores of Italy.[59]

The bow used by Scythians and Cimmerians was no ordinary composite bow. It is small compared with later bows used on the steppe[60] and is made of horn or wood[61] and strung with animal tendon or horsehair.[62] Horsehair may have been the Scythians' preferred material for stringing the bow. Horsehair is better than animal tendon strings, which tend to stretch if they absorb moisture in colder climates, such as the steppe.[63] Stringing the bow was a difficult process. In order to string the bow, a Scythian archer must utilize both legs and arms as shown in Figure 10. According to the Greek mythological tale of Hercules and his three sons, the son who can string and bend the bow can stay in the land, but those sons who cannot string the bow will have to leave the land and go somewhere else. Both the oldest and middle sons could not string the bow, but Scythes, Hercules youngest son, bent and strung the bow and is allowed to stay in the land that is named after him.[64] The arms of the bow curved outward from the handle grip resembling a "Cupid's bow."[65] Strabo compares the bow's shape to the Black Sea.[66] The tips of bow lacked ears, giving it more flexibility.[67] The length of the Scythian bow is approximately 80 cm (2.6 feet) in length,[68] while other bows found in burial mounds at Pazyryk, Russia, measured 127 centimeters (4.2 feet).[69] Overall, the Scythian double-curved composite bow is small, stiff, hardy, and powerful. But how far could the bow deliver an arrow?

Figure 14 Scythian stringing his bow on the right[70]

There is an old Greek grave at a place called Olbia, a former Greek colony on the Black Sea, which is located on the Dnieper-Bug estuary.[71] The inscription on the grave, which is short and dated generally around 300 BCE states, "Anaxagoras son of Dimagoras shot an arrow from his bow to a range of 282 orgyiai." The arrow delivered traveled 521.6 meters (1711.282 feet), which is a little more than 567 yards according to the inscription.[72] This is an incredible distance to say the least, but in combat, the Scythians had to be effective and accurate when concentrating on a single target, unless the target was a massive army, in which case you need only to hit someone at random (e.g., The Battle of Carrhae, 53 BCE).

For a Scythian archer to be effective in killing or wounding his enemy, he had to be at a distance of 160 yards; however to be lethal, he had to be at least 160 to 200 feet away. In addition, they would carry anywhere between 30, 150,[73] and some estimates say up to 200[74] arrows in their quivers. When engaged in combat, the archer could release up to 12 arrows a minute,[75] while others suggest 20 arrows a minute,[76] but of course, this would depend on the nature of the battle.

The Scythians were not necessarily looking for one shot, one kill. I am sure they would take advantage if the opportunity presented itself. The Scythians in battle would position their bows at a 45-degree angle. From this angle, they would shower the enemy with arrows to kill if possible, but mutilation would be the main objective from such a distance. Arrows from this distance would fall erratically on top of the enemy. Due to the distance of the shot, the intention would be to demoralize the enemy in hope that the enemy forces would withdraw. If the enemy withdrew, the Scythian horse archers could begin to pick apart their enemy with individual kill method, or leave him alone entirely. Not a bad method, it shows us one of many reasons why those who encountered them so dearly desired their bow.[77]

An example of this raining death is at the Battle of Carrhae in 53 BCE between Rome and Parthia. Dr. Kaveh Farrokh suggests that the average Parthian horse archer, with a quiver of 30 arrows, loosed between 8-10 arrows a minute at Carrhae. It would take 2-3 minutes to exhaust his arsenal before needing resupplied. The amount of Parthian horse archers at the battle is estimated at 10,000. Now, if all 10,000 fired away for 20 minutes, the amount of arrows fired by an individual horse archer would have been between 160-200 arrows. Take 10,000 and the amount of arrows fired upon the Roman soldiers are estimated to have been an astounding 1.6-2 million arrows in a 20-minute timeframe.[78]

The Scythian bow was the AK-47 of the Ancient Near East and the weapon of choice to dominate the battlefield. Even though the bow is unique and designed to deliver the utmost damage, the arrow the bow delivered was even nastier! Scythians uniquely designed their arrowheads for maximum penetration of the opponent's armor. Beyond that, Scythian arrowheads were extremely poisonous. Before we pick our poison, we must pick our point.

The Scythian arrowhead, also known as a "Scythian point," is of a trilobate shape.[79] The design of the arrowhead is like a rocket or bullet with three blades protruding from the body. Some of the arrowheads had protruding barbs, while others did not.[80] The trilobate was usually made of bronze. The shaft used to deliver arrowhead was made of reed or wood, roughly 30 inches long.[81] The design and craftsmanship in producing such an arrowhead is brilliant, for its aerodynamic body makes it practical to use against the finest and toughest of armor.

The Scythian point originated around the 7th century BCE. This could suggest that Scythians developed a point in order to pierce Assyrian armor at the time in question. Scythians and Cimmerians were indeed at war with Assyria off and on during the 7th century BCE.[82] Now, this is not the only arrowhead style or metal used by the Scythians, for some arrowheads were made of bone, stone, iron, and bronze. As for shape, some looked like small spearheads,[83] while others are leaf-shaped, which may have been used for hunting; others are trilobite shape as discussed, most likely used for combat purposes.[84]

Besides the lethal design of the Scythian trilobite point, another nasty feature was the use of poison. Not only were they experts at archery, but also biological warfare. The land the Scythians inhabit is home to a number of snakes from which they draw venom. Such snakes inhabiting the area included the steppe viper, Caucasus viper, European adder, and the long-nose/sand viper.[85] The Scythians had a vast arsenal of snake venoms of all degrees at their disposal. The book titled, *"On Marvelous Things Heard,"* by Pseudo-Aristotle, which was a work written by his followers if not written in part by Aristotle himself, mentions the Scythian handling of snakes and how to extract their poison:

> They say that the Scythian poison, in which that people dips its arrows, is procured from the viper. The Scythians, it would appear, watch those that are just bringing forth young, and take them, and allow them to putrefy for some days.

After several days passed, the Scythian shaman would then take the venom and mix it with other ingredients. One of these concoctions required human blood:

But when the whole mass appears to them to have become sufficiently rotten, they pour human blood into a little pot, and, after covering it with a lid, bury it in a dung-hill. And when this likewise has putrefied, they mix that which settles on the top, which is of a watery nature, with the corrupted blood of the viper, and thus make it a deadly poison.[86]

The Roman author Aelian also mentions this process, saying, "The Scythians are even said to mix serum from the human body with the poison that they smear upon their arrows."[87] Both accounts show the Scythians were able to excite the blood in order to separate it from the yellow watery plasma. Once the mixture of blood and dung had putrefied, the shaman would take the serum and excrement and mix it in with the next ingredient, venom, along with the decomposed viper. Once the process is complete, the Scythians would place their arrowheads into this deadly mixture ready for use.[88] The historian Strabo mentions a second use of this deadly poison:

> The Soanes use poison of an extraordinary kind for the points of their weapons; even the odour of this poison is a cause of suffering to those who are wounded by arrows thus prepared.[89]

I suppose one could get used to the reek after being around it day in and day out. On the other hand, the poisonous fragrance might take longer to get accustomed to, especially the receiver of the arrow, since all things deadly are alive and well on the tip of an arrowhead.

Even though the arrowhead is poisonous, the barbs on the arrowhead are sometimes poisonous as well. The Roman poet Ovid, who was exiled to the Black Sea, got a good look at these poisonous barbs and describes them as "native arrow-points have their steel barbs smeared with poison, carry a double hazard of death." He also describes the poisonous ingredient as "yellow with vipers gall."[90] To get a better understanding of this "double death," Renate Rolle elaborates further on the barbed arrowheads: "These arrowheads, fitted with hooks and soaked in poison, were particularly feared, since they were very difficult to remove from the wound and caused the victim great pain during the process."[91] A very grim picture without question, too be struck by an arrowhead with barbs or hooks that is poisoned with putrefied remains are indeed horrific. However, I wonder if the Scythian archers used different types of poisons on each individual barb or hook besides the main poison on the point itself.

With all these different poisons used by the Scythians, they had to know how to tell what was what in their gorytus. This gorytus is the case that held the bow and quiver of arrows. The length of the gorytas is relatively shorter than the bow itself, leaving the bow partially exposed. The gorytas also had a metal covering for the arrows.[92] This is most likely to protect the archer from scraping his skin across the poisonous arrowheads. The Scythians would paint their arrow shafts in the color of red or black, while others had zigzag and diamond patters painted upon them. These various patterns painted upon the arrow shafts are the same patterns found upon the various vipers used by the Scythians as their agents of death. Vipers with a zigzag or diamond pattern upon their backs are the most poisonous of all. Adrienne Mayor, on page 84 of her book, *"Greek Fire, Poison Arrows & Scorpion Bombs,"* illustrates the various snake patterns used by the Scythians. The painted design is a way for the archer to tell which poison he is using. I also agree with Mayor that the painted arrow shafts, when fired at the enemy, likely had a psychological effect, for they must have looked like snakes flying through the air, while the barbs protruding from the point may have looked like fangs to the enemy.[93]

Figure 15 Scythian Archers[94]

Figure 16 Scythian Trilobate Arrowheads courtesy of Sergi from Metal Detecting World.com [95]

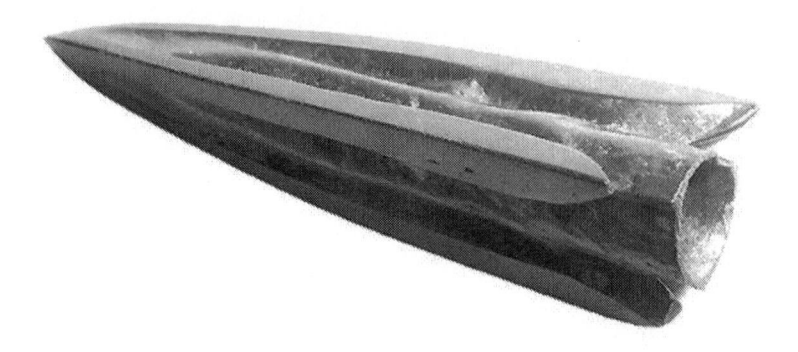

Shield

The Scythians carried small shields, for the most part. The shield utilized was round and a little over a foot in diameter -- not big by any standard.[96] The Scythians did carry much larger shields of various shapes as shown on Figure 1. Other shapes include the crescent shape that the Greeks depict in some of their artwork.[97] The shields were made of wood for the most part[98] and covered with iron plates[99] or reindeer skin.[100] Some of the shields are just plain, no image of any kind, while other shields had decorations of deer or fish, which seemed to be the image of choice, but other animal images were used as well.[101]

The practicality of the shields' size is important, for a small shield does not hinder the rider in performing his actions when loosing his arrows, which is likely repositioned to his back during engagements. On the other hand, the shield would be useful to the rider on foot if his horse were cut down from underneath him when engaging the enemy. However, the size of shield shows us that the typical Scythian horse archer is not made for heavy infantry close combat, unless all other options have been exhausted. The same might be said of the heavy cavalryman, since their role is to puncture holes through the enemy lines, as in the description of the Massagetae provided by Herodotus,[102] or the description Plutarch provides about the Parthians at Carrhae.[103] Both historians descriptions suggest that if a heavy cavalryman is knocked off his horse, he is not capable of protecting himself efficiently due to the weight of the armor.

Endnotes: Appendix I

[1] Herodotus, *The Histories* 1. 215.
[2] Justin, *Epitome* 41.2
[3] Tadeusz Sulimirski, *The Sarmations* (London: Thomas & Hudson, 1970), 31.
[4] Gabriel, *The Great Armies of Antiquity*, 21.
[5] Antony Karasulas, *Mounted Archers of the Steppe 600 BC-AD 1300* (Oxford: Osprey Publishing, 2004), 29-30
[6] E.V. Cernenko and Angus McBride, *The Scythians 700-300 B.C.* (Oxford: Osprey Publishing, 1983), 7.
[7] Ibid., 7
[8] Ibid., 8
[9] Edith Hamilton, Mythology (Boston: Little Brown and Company, 1942), 201.
[10] Herodotus, *The Histories* 4.20,56.
[11] Plutarch, and Robin Seager. *The Fall of the Roman Republic: Six Lives (Penguin Classics). Revised ed.* London: Penguin Classics, 1984), 142-144.
[12] Scythian comb. Soloha kurgan. Hermitage museum, St. Petersburg, Russia. http://commons.wikimedia.org/wiki/File:Scythian_comb.jpg
[13] Parthian horsemen - Septimus Severus, McClintock & Strong Encyclopedia
[14] Esther Jacobson, *The Art of the Scythians: The Interpenetration of Cultures at the Edge of the Hellenic World (Handbook of Oriental Studies, Vol 2* (Koninklijke Brill NV, Leiden, The Netherlands: Brill Academic Publishers, 1995), 160.
[15] Burchard Brentjes, *Arms of the Sakas: And Other Tribes of the Central Asian Republics* (Kfar Sava: Rishi Publications, 1996), 58.
[16] Renate Rolle, *The World of the Scythians* (Berkeley: University of California Press, 1989), 69.
[17] Arrian, *Anabasis* (3.13.4)
[18] Burchard Brentjes, *Arms of the Sakas: And Other Tribes of the Central Asian Republics* (Kfar Sava: Rishi Publications, 1996), 58.
[19] Elena E. Kuz'mina, J. P. Mallory, *The Origin of the Indo-Iranians, Volume 3* (Leiden: Brill, 2007), 399.
[20] Tamas Dezso, *Oriental influence in the Aegean and Eastern Mediterranean helmet traditions in the 9th-7th centuries B.C.* (London: British Archaeological Reports, 1998), 13, 45.
[21] Sir Austen Henry Layard, *Nineveh and Its Remains: With an account of a visit to the Chaldæan christians of Kurdistan, and the Yezidis, or*

devil-worshippers; and an enquiry into ... and arts of the ancient Assyrians (New York: D. Appleton and Company, 1858), 262.
[22] Farrokh, 30, note 87.
[23] Jona Lendering, "The Saka Tigrakhauda relief of the eastern stairs at Persepolis." 2005. na, Amsterdam. *www.livius.org*. Web. 3 Sept. 2012.
[24] Karen J. Hatzigeorgiou, "Assyrian Soldiers." 2012. http://karenswhimsy.com/assyrians.shtm. Web. 3 Sept. 2012.
[25] Herodotus, *The Histories* 1.215; 7. 64.
[26] Xenophon, *Anabasis* 4.4.16.
[27] Erik Hildinger, *Warriors of the Steppe: A Military History of Central Asia, 500 B.C. to A.D. 1700* (New York and Washington D.C.: Da Capo Press, 2001), 35
[28] Michael Rostovtzeff, *Iranians & Greeks in South Russia* London: Oxford University Press, 1922), 58-59.
[29] Euphronios, "Scythian Archer." 14 December 2007. Louvre Museum, Paris, France, *http://en.wikipedia.org/wiki/File:Skythian_archer_Louvre_G106.jpg*. Web, 3 Sept. 2012.
[30] Cernenko and McBride, 17.
[31] Ellis H. Minns, *Scythians and Greeks* (New York: Biblo and Tannen, 1971), 68, 319. (See Fig 223,230.
[32] Herodotus, *The Histories* 1. 214.
[33] Muhammad. A. Dandamaev, *A Political History of the Achaemenid Empire* (Leiden: Brill Academic Publishers, 1990), 10.
[34] Herodotus, *The Histories* 1. 215.
[35] Tadeusz Sulimirski, *The Sarmations*, 31.
[36] George Rawlinson, *The Sixth Great Oriental Monarchy: Or the Geography, History & Antiquities of Parthia* (London: Longmans, Green, and Co., 1873), 389.
[37] Virgil, *Aeneid* 8.965.
[38] Simon Anglim, Rob S. Rice, Phyllis G. Jestice, Scott Rusch, John Serrati, *Fighting Techniques of the Ancient World (3000 B.C. to 500 A.D.): Equipment, Combat Skills, and Tactics* (New York: Thomas Dunne Books, 2003), 96.
[39] Tamara Talbot Rice, *The Scythians* (New York: Praeger, 1957), 127.
[40] Minns, 68.
[41] Cernenko and McBride, 17.
[42] Minns, 68.
[43] Jeannine Davis-Kimball, Vladimir A. Bashilov, and Leonid T. Yablonsky, *Nomads of the Eurasian Steppes in the Early Iron Age* (Berkeley, CA: ZINAT PRESS, 1995), 15.

[44] Cernenko and McBride, 17, 19.
[45] Terrence Poulos, Extreme *War: The Biggest, Best, Bloodiest, and Worst in Warfare* (New York: Citadel), 33.
[46] Herodotus, *The Histories 4, 9-10, 62.*
[47] Lucian, *Toxaris* 38.
[48] Minns, 68.
[49] Herodotus, *The Histories* 3.118, 7.54./ Flavius Josephus, *Antiquity of the Jews* 20.185.
[50] Herodotus, *The Histories* 8.120.
[51] Xenophon, *Anabasis* 1.2.27.
[52] Xenophon, *Anabasis* 1.8.29.
[53] Ada Bruhn de Hoffmeyer, "Introduction to the History of the European Swords," *Gladius* Vol 1. (1961): 53-55.
[54] Franz Valéry Marie Cumont, *The Mysteries of Mithra* (London: Kegan Paul, Trench, Trubner & Co., LTD, 1903), 176.
[55] August Baumeister, "Darius from builder: the monuments of classical Alterums. 1885th Volume I, Table VI. The figure shows the so-called Greek Darius Darius vase in Naples, found in 1851 in Canosa." 11 September 2005. *http://en.wikipedia.org/wiki/File:Darius-Vase.jpg*. Web, 3 Sept. 2012.
[56] G. Maspero, *History of Egypt, Chaldea, Syria, Babylonia, and Assyria, Volume VIII, Part B* (London: The Grolier Society Publishers, 1903), 240.
[57] Anthony M. Snodgrass, *Arms and Armor of the Greeks* (Baltimore: The Johns Hopkins University Press, 1998), 99.
[58] Plato, *Laws* (New York: Akasha Classics, 2009), 357.
[59] Howard L. Blackmore, *Hunting Weapons from the Middle Ages to the Twentieth Century* (New York: Dover Publications; Dover Ed edition, 2000), 120.
[60] Hildinger, 36.
[61] Cernenko and McBride, 11.
[62] Bhupinder Singh Mahal, *Punjab: The Nomads and The Mavericks* (New Delhi: Sunbun Publishers, 2000), 30.
[63] Karasulas, 21.
[64] Herodotus. *The Histories*, 4. 9-10.
[65] Hildinger, 36.
[66] Minns, 66.
[67] Hildinger, 36.
[68] Cernenko and McBride, 11.
[69] Heidi Knecht, *Projectile Technology* (New York: Springer, 1997), 153.

[70] "Scythian warriors, drawn after figures on an electrum cup from the Kul'Oba kurgan burial near Kerch." Photograph. 1900. Hermitage Museum, St Petersburg. *http://en.wikipedia.org/wiki/File:Scythian_Warriors.jpg*. Web. 3 Sept. 2012.
[71] Cernenko and McBride, 12.
[72] Karasulas, 23.
[73] Ibid.
[74] James R. Ashley, *The Macedonian Empire: The Era of Warfare Under Philip II and Alexander the Great, 359-323 B.C.* (Jefferson, N.C.: Mcfarland & Company, 2004), 66.
[75] Karasulas, 23.
[76] Adrienne Mayor, *Greek Fire, Poison Arrows & Scorpion Bombs* (Woodstock & New York: Overlook Duckworth, 2003), 85-86.
[77] Karasulas, 23.
[78] Farrokh, 133.
[79] McMurray, Heather. "AN IRON II SCYTHIAN POINT FROM KHIRBAT AL-MUDAYBIC." Virtual Karak Resources Project. Appalachian College Association. 22 Nov. 2003. http://www.vkrp.org/studies/historical/scythian-point/... (accessed May 04, 2010).
[80] Karasulas, 22
[81] Minns, 68.
[82] McMurray, Heather. "AN IRON II SCYTHIAN POINT FROM KHIRBAT AL-MUDAYBIC." Virtual Karak Resources Project. Appalachian College Association. 22 Nov. 2003. http://www.vkrp.org/studies/historical/scythian-point/... (accessed May 04, 2010).
[83] Minns, 68.
[84] McMurray, Heather. "AN IRON II SCYTHIAN POINT FROM KHIRBAT AL-MUDAYBIC." Virtual Karak Resources Project. Appalachian College Association. 22 Nov. 2003. http://www.vkrp.org/studies/historical/scythian-point/... (accessed May 04, 2010).
[85] Mayor, 80.
[86] Pseudo-Aristotle, *On Marvelous Things Heard or De mirabilibus auscultationibus,*trans. J.A. Smith & W. D. Ross (Oxford: Clarendon Press, 1909), 845 a 5 (141)
[87] Aelian, Alwyn Faber Scholfield, *On the characteristics of animals Vol 2* (New York: Harvard University Press, 1959), 235.
[88] Mayor, 81.

[89] Strabo's, *Geography Book 11.2.19,* trans. W. Falconer (London: George Bell & Sons, 1903, 229.
[90] Ovid, Peter Green, *The poems of exile: Tristia and the Black Sea letters* (Berkeley: University of California Press, 2005), 95, 182.
[91] Rolle, 65.
[92] Cernenko and McBride, 12
[93] Mayor, 83-85.
[94] "Scythian Bowmen." Photograph. 19 February 2007. State Hermitage Museum, St. Petersburg, http://en.wikipedia.org/wiki/File:Bowmena.PNG.Web, 3 Sept. 2012.
[95] Sergi, "Scythian Bronze Armor-Piercing Trilobated Arrowhead, ca 600-300 B.C.," Photograph. http://metaldetectingworld.com/ http://metaldetectingworld.com/06_finds_scythian_arrowhead.shtml. Web, 5 Sept. 2012.
[96] Rice, 127.
[97] Esther Jacobson, *The art of the Scythians: the interpenetration of cultures at the edge of the Hellenic world*, 160.
[98] Rice, 127.
[99] Rolle, 68.
[100] Minns, 73.
[101] Ibid., 73.
[102] Herodotus, *The Histories* 1. 215.
[103] Plutarch and Robin Seager. *The Fall of the Roman Republic: Six Lives*, 142-144.

Appendix II

Tactics

The Scythians may not be the original inventors of asymmetrical warfare, but one could argue that they perfected it. Before and during the Scythian arrival, many nations fought by conventional methods. In other words, the established civilizations of Assyria, Babylonia, and Persia, used taxes to feed, equip, and maintain their large armies. Overall, one can see the massive expense it is to arm and defend a nation when war comes a-knocking. Lives and money are lost, doubly so if you go on the offensive at the expense of your nation's pocket.

The Scythians, on the other hand, needed none of these, for they were tribal based and seemed to come together only in a time of war. Thus, most issues did not hinder them, such as the laws of supply and demand in the military economical sense, which would affect an established kingdom or empire. The land was their supplier and demand was when they were in need of resources. For Scythians to sustain life, they had to move to new regions in search of ample pastures suited for their horses to graze and abundant with game, while the land they moved from was left to rest. But one has to be cautious as well, for even though the Scythians moved around, many stayed within their tribal territory. In some cases, they ventured into another tribal territory due to the need to sustain life for both tribe and livestock.[1]

When one examines the Scythian lifestyle, one can easily gain an understanding of the type of warfare necessarily carried on against more sedentary (non-migratory) people, like those in Mesopotamia. The Scythian took a guerilla approach to warfare as their method, not to be confused with terrorism. The term guerrilla warfare means irregular warfare and its doctrine advocates for the use of small bands to conduct military operations. Herodotus mentions their method of warfare when King Darius of Persia campaigned against them.

> It is thus with me, Persian: I have never fled for fear of any man, nor do I now flee from you; this that I have done is no new thing or other than my practice in peace. But as to the reason why I do not straightway fight with you, this too I will tell you. For we Scythians have no towns or planted lands, that we might meet you the sooner in battle, fearing lest the one be taken or the other wasted. But if nothing will serve you but fighting straightway, we have the graves of our fathers; come, find these and essay to destroy them; then shall you know whether we will fight you for those graves or no. Till

then we will not join battle unless we think it good.[2]

The description indicates that the Scythians against whom Darius is warring have no center of gravity; more on this later.

Swarming

The Scythians are best known for swarming the enemy, like at the Battle of Carrhae in 53 BCE, where they demonstrated this tactic during the initial stages of the attack. The swarming tactic is the first stage before any other mechanism is executed, like feinting or defense in depth.

To summarize, the definition of swarming would be a battle involving several or more units pouncing on an intended target simultaneously.[3] The whole premise of swarming in guerrilla warfare, as indicated in the U.S. Army Field Manual (FM) 90-8 on the topic of *counterguerrilla operations,* is to locate, fix, and engage the enemy, but to avoid larger forces,[4] unless you possess units capable of countering the other. This would allow other units to take advantage of the enemy, which is rare in most battles involving the Scythians. The key principle of swarming is that it does not matter if you win the battle so long as you do not lose the war. It is designed to disorient the enemy troops.

The swarming tactic comprises many units converging on the intended target; however, the swarm moves with the target in order to fracture it. Thus, the method of swarming is to dislodge the enemy piecemeal, causing rank and file to implode. This is due to longstanding, snail-like movement during battle, meantime being continuously pelted from afar by projectiles; fear takes over, demoralizing an army. Roman soldiers were to have a taste of this, for they had a space of three feet all around them to allow for movement and maneuvering in battle. The Scythians took advantage of their three feet,[5] as Plutarch mentions, at the battle of Carrhae: "Huddled together in a narrow space and getting into each other's way, they were shot down by arrows."[6] The heavy barrage of arrows would cause some to wander off, bit-by-bit, thus allowing horse archers to concentrate fully on the wandering enemy. In this scenario, one can argue that the initial battle tactic is to pelt the enemy with a volley of arrows, keeping the target tight in order to fracture it, which allows the horse archers to go from random pelting to accurately killing the enemy. In other words, they switch from firing up into the air to firing forward at the enemy, as demonstrated at Carrhae in 53 BCE.[7]

Now, before we go any further, let me briefly make the case that swarming has many different methods or tactics, but the Scythian swarm is not like that of others. However, a swarm is a swarm, but the method varies. Case in point, "mass swarming" is the most sought- after method in both the ancient and medieval world, demonstrated by massive conventional armies that would eventually separate or disassemble and perform convergent attacks over a region or province from its initial phase. The "dispersed swarm" is the preferred tactic in guerrilla warfare, where the body separates and converges on the battlefield without forming a single body.[8]

The whole premise of swarming in guerilla warfare is to engage quickly but to avoid larger forces. Pharnuches, one of Alexander's generals, made the fatal mistake by falling for the Scythian feinting tactic, in which he chased after the Scythians, only to find himself ambushed and swarmed. Pharnuches should have never been given command, because he was a diplomat, not an experienced officer.[9]

The Battle of Jaxartes is a fine example of the swarming tactic, but rather small in scale. The Scythians harassing the forces of Alexander did not appear to be a large force. Rather, the Scythians at the battle intended to demoralize the enemy, and if that did not work, they could always lead the enemy farther inland and begin the strategy of defense in depth. Alexander knew better after he defeated the Scythians at Jaxartes in 329 BCE.[10] Alexander understood quite well that if he were to pursue the Scythians further inland, his forces would be open to hit and run attacks, famine, and psychological attrition, none of which is desirable. Even Alexander understood the limits of empire, especially when his worldview did not incorporate the lands to the north.

The Battle of Jaxartes was a loss for the Scythians and a victory for the Macedonians. However, two important demonstrations of the tactics are visible at the battle. The first tactic is swarming, the second is what I like to call the swarm-anti-swarm tactic developed by Alexander, commonly referred to as "anti-swarming." In fact, Alexander had to swarm in order to achieve victory. The swarm-anti-swarm counters the enemy with a bait-unit. Once the enemy converged from several sides, the remainder of the forces will converge on the area and swarm the enemy. Alexander learned quickly to adopt this tactic of closing in on the enemy and attacking from all directions for future use.[11]

Feinting

Scythian tactics included feinting or withdrawing from either the battlefield or even the region. An example of feinting comes from a battle mentioned earlier, the battle of Carrhae in 53 BCE.

The Roman historian Plutarch mentions that the Parthian horse archers would not engage the Roman forces during battle, but would retreat, luring the Roman forces to follow. The trap was set and the Romans thought victory was in hand, until the fleeing horse archers turned and loosed arrows upon the pursuing Romans. The Romans in the pursuit soon realized they had made a terrible mistake, but it was too late. Nothing could be done but to make a defensive stand. Withdrawal allowed the feinting tactic to be used with proficiency due to Roman ignorance of their enemy. The Romans would try to advance, but with every attempt, the Parthian horse archers' constant pelting with what seemed to be an endless supply of arrows would keep them in place. Parthian camel units resupplied the horse archers by exchanging empty quivers for full ones, then and returning to their position. During this monotonous, never-ending event, the Romans would try to break the horse archer formations, only to be countered by heavy Parthian cavalry known as (cataphract), which acted as the anvil to the Parthian hammer (arrows). The Battle of Carrhae was death by pieces for the Romans.[12]

Therefore, when it comes to the feinting tactic, do not watch for the visible hand, but rather the invisible one. The Parthians and Scythians were notoriously successful in the feinting technique before the battle of Carrhae. Afterward, the countering measure to this tactic went largely ignored until Alexander the Great demonstrated a reversal.

One could make the argument that the Romans had faulty intelligence before Carrhae, but this would be unfair, although true to a certain extent. The truth of the matter is that the Romans invaded a land they did not know, looking to conquer a people they did not understand. In the end, both Rome and Parthia would continue to bash each other as the years turned into centuries, but neither side truly dominated the other.

Defense in Depth

Defense in Depth is most successful if your nation is rather large and unproductive as in the case of the Scythians, who valued land and the ability to roam, rather than the luxuries of the cities, like Athens or Nineveh. The Scythians did seem to have cities or mobile villages, which may be a more correct term. As for the lazy luxuries of life, some settled, but the majority roamed about.

According to Herodotus: "We Scythians have neither towns nor cultivated lands, which might induce us, through fear of their being taken or ravaged, to be in any hurry to fight with you."[13] But Herodotus also states: "Having neither cities nor forts, and carrying their dwellings with them wherever they go; accustomed, moreover, one and all of them, to shoot from horseback; and living not by husbandry but on their cattle, their wagons the only houses that they possess."[14] The Scythians did have slaves, according to Herodotus, who were blind and whose primary task was being a shepherd.[15] Additionally, Herodotus also mentions Scythians who grew corn and onions, which indicates that agriculture was common among some of the tribes.[16] Therefore, the notion that the Scythians did not have cities/villages is partially untrue, depending on the Scythic tribe, of course.

The Scythians that Darius the Great attacked did not have cultivated lands or towns that could be beneficial to Darius' forces. The Scythians conducted a scorched earth policy as Darius's army marched further inland, following after them. The Scythians understood that an army marches on its belly and so do the animals accompanying them. What Darius could not use would be a weapon against his forces. The strategy would be defense in depth, scorched earth policy the tactic, and the outcome would be starvation. Starvation through burning was the preferred method used to rid of the Persians. The Scythians understood that they could defeat the enemy by allowing the land to swallow them both physically and mentally.

Darius was ignorant of the people he wished to conquer; he shows no knowledge of the people or terrain he is about to invade. Because of this attitude by Darius, his brother, Artabanus, warned that the proposed campaign to conquer the European Scythians was far too risky, and even if it was successful, the economic benefits were limited. Nevertheless, Darius had to learn the hard way. For the Scythians, it was a good way to prevent a possible second invasion.

As mentioned, the Scythians used the land to their advantage, knowing that Darius would follow as long as the bait was present. The Scythians burnt all that grew, causing Darius to follow his enemy across burnt terrain in hopes of finding food for both his men and animals. The Scythians began hit and run attacks during mealtime and even at night, preventing the men from eating or even sleeping, irritating them even more. The Scythians knew that as long as Darius followed in pursuit, he would gain nothing, not even an engagement. Psychological and physical attrition would set in by attacking the enemy's stomach and his need for rest, causing irrationality among the troops and further deteriorating the chain of command.[17]

In the end, the Scythians won a great victory by not engaging the enemy in conventional warfare, but beat the Persians through starvation and sleep deprivation, since an army can move only for so long before it needs to fuel up again in both rest and food. By denying both, the Scythians utilized a form of defense in depth that saved them from Persian conquest.

Endnotes: Appendix II

[1] Ian Morris, *Why the West rules--for Now: the Patterns of History, and What They Reveal About the Future* (New York: Farrar, Straus and Giroux, 2010), 277-279.

[2] Herodotus, *The Histories*, 4. 127.

[3] Sean J.A. Edwards, *Swarming on the Battlefield: Past, Present, and Future*, (Santa Monica: Rand Corporation, 2000), xii.

[4] U.S. Department of Defense, *Counterguerrilla Operations*, (Washington DC: Department of the Army, FM 90-8, August 1986), Chapter 4, Section III. 4-10.

[5] Polybius. 18.30.6

[6] Plutarch, Crassus, 25.5

[7] Farrokh,133.

[8] Sean J.A. Edwards, *Swarming on the Battlefield: Past, Present, and Future*, xiii

[9] John Frederick Charles Fuller, *The Generalship of Alexander the Great*, (New York and Washington D.C.: Da Capo Press, 2004), 118-120.

[10] Edwards, 14-20.

[11] Ibid.

[12] Plutarch, Crassus, 24.5.

[13] Herodotus, *The Histories*, 4.127.

[14] Ibid, 4.46.

[15] Ibid, 4.2.

[16] Ibid, 4.17.

[17] Ibid, 4.122-134.

Bibliography

"Helmet of Assyrian horseman." Drawn from bas-relief of Nineveh, B.C. 700. Photograph. http://www.biblehistory.com/ibh/Weapons+and+Warfare/Helmets/Helmet+Of+Assyrian+Horseman. Web. 3 Sept. 2012.

"Manna,"Photograph.http://az.wikipedia.org/http://az.wikipedia.org/wiki/%C5%9E%C9%99kil:Manna_ilkin_yaranma_v%C9%99_geni%C5%9Fl%C9%99nm%C9%99.jpg. 11 August 2009. Web, 5 Sept. 2012.

"Scythian Bowmen." Photograph. 19 February 2007. State Hermitage Museum, St. Petersburg, http://en.wikipedia.org/wiki/File:Bowmena.PNG.Web, 3 Sept. 2012.

Anderson, Jeff S. *The Internal Diversification of Second Temple Judaism: An Introduction to the Second Temple Period*. Lanham, MD: University Press of America, 2002.

Anglim, Simon, Phyllis Jestice, Rob S. Rice, Scott Rusch, and John Serrati. *Fighting Techniques of the Ancient World (3000 B.C. to 500 A.D.): Equipment, Combat Skills, and Tactics*. New York: Thomas Dunne Books, 2003.

Aristotle, trans. Smith, J.A., Ross, W.D. *On Marvelous Things Heard or De mirabilibus auscultationibus*. Oxford: Clarendon Press, 1909.

Arrian. *Anabasis*.

Arrianus, Flavius. Arrian. *Anabasis of Alexander, Books 5-7. Indica. / with an Engl. transl. by P.A. Brunt.- Revised text and translation with new introd., notes and appendices ed.* Cambridge, Mass: Harvard University Press, 1983.

Ashley, James R. *Macedonian Empire: The Era of Warfare Under Philip II and Alexander the Great, 359-323 B.C.* Jefferson, N.C.: Mcfarland & Company, 2004.

Ashrafian, Hutan. "Limb gigantism, neurofibromatosis and royal heredity in the Ancient World 2500 years ago: Achaemenids and Parthians." *Journal of Plastic, Reconstructive & Aesthetic Surgery Volume 64, Issue 4*, 2011: 557.

Assar, G.R.F. "A Revised Parthian Chronology of the Period 165-91 B.C." In *Electrum: Greek and Hellenistic Studies vol. 11*, by Edward Dabrowa, 81-149. Krakow: Jagiellonian University Press, 2006.

Asthana, N. C. and Anjali Nirmal. *Urban terrorism: Myths and Realities*. Jaipur: 2009, Pointer Publishers.

Athenaeus of Naucratis, translated by Charles Duke Yonge. *The Deipnosophists, or, Banquet of the learned of Athenaeus, Volume 1*. Oxford: Henry G. Bohn, 1854.

Azzaroli, Augusto. *An Early History of Horsemanship*. Brill/W. Backhuys: Leiden: E.J., 1985.

Bar-Kochva, Bezalel. *The Seleucid Army: Organization and Tactics in the Great Campaigns*. Cambridge : Cambridge University Press, 1976.

Baumeister, August "Darius from builder: the monuments of classical Alterums. 1885th Volume I, Table VI. The figure shows the so-called Greek Darius Darius vase in Naples, found in 1851 in Canosa." 11 September 2005. http://en.wikipedia.org/wiki/File:Dari.

Beal, Timothy Kandler. *Religion and its Monsters*. New York: Routledge, 2002.

Bevan, Edwyn Robert. *House of Seleucus (2 Volumes in 1)*. Ares Publishers , Jan 1985.

Bivar, A. D. H. "Cavalry Equipment and Tactics on the Euphrates Frontier." *Dumbarton Oaks Papers , Vol. 26*, 1972: 271-291.

Blackmore, Howard L. *Hunting Weapons from the Middle Ages to the Twentieth Century: With 288 Illustrations*. New York: Dover Publications, 2000.

Blenkinsopp, Joseph. *A History of prophecy in Israel*. Philadelphia: Westminster Press, 1996.

Boardman, John, I. E. S. Edwards, E. Sollberger, N. G. L. Hammond. *The Cambridge Ancient History, Volume 3,*

Part 2: The Assyrian and Babylonian Empires and Other States of the Near East, from the Eighth to the Sixth Centuries BC. Cambridge: Cambridge University Press, 1991.

Bockting, Walter O., and Eli Coleman. *Gender Dysphoria: Interdisciplinary Approaches in Clinical Management.* New York: Hayworth Press, 1993.

Boyce, Mary. *A history of Zoroastrianism.* Leiden: E.J. Brill, 1982.

Brentjes, Burchard. *Arms of the Sakas: And Other Tribes of the Central Asian Republics.* Kfar Sava: Rishi Publications, 1996.

Briant, Pierre. *From Cyrus to Alexander: A History of the Persian Empire.* Winona Lake, Indiana: Eisenbrauns, 2002.

Brosius, Maria. *Women in Ancient Persia, 559-331 B.C. .* Oxford: Clarendon, 1998.

Budge, Sir E. A. Wallis. *The History of Esarhaddon: Son of Sennacherib king of Assyria Bc 681 to 668. 1880. Reprint.* New York: Kessinger Publishing, 2005.

Çambel, Halet and John David Hawkins. *Corpus of Hieroglyphic Luwian Inscriptions: Inscriptions of the Iron Age.* Berlin: Walter de Gruyter, 2000.

Capt, E. Raymond. *Missing Links Discovered in Assyrian Tablets.* Thousand Oaks: Artisan Sales, 1985.

Cernenko, E. V. McBride, Angus. *The Scythians 700-300 B.C.* Oxford: Osprey Publishing, 1983.

Chahin, M. *The Kingdom of Armenia.* New York: Dorset Press, 1991.

Chavalas, Mark William. *The Ancient Near East: Historical Sources in Translation.* Malden, MA: Blackwell, 2006.

Ctesias, and Jan P. Stronk. *Ctesias' Persian history.* Dusseldorf: Wellem, 2010.

Cumont, Franz Valéry Marie. *The Mysteries of Mithra.* London: Kegan Paul, Trench, Trubner & Co., LTD, 1903.

—. *The Mysteries of Mithra.* London: Kegan Paul, Trench, Trubner & Co., LTD, 1903.

Curtis, Stewart, and Sarah Stewart. *The Age of the Parthians The Idea of Iran Volume II.* London: I.B.Tauris & Co Ltd, 2007.

Dandamaev, Muhammad A., and Vladimir G. Lukonin. *The culture and social institutions of ancient Iran.* Cambridge UK: Cambridge University Press, 2004.

Dandamaev, Muhammad A., Vladimir G. Lukonin, Philip L. Kohl, and D. J. Dadson. *The Culture and Social Institutions of Ancient Iran.* New York: Cambridge University Press, 2004.

Dandamaey, Muhammad A. *Political History of the Achaemenid Empire.* Leiden: Brill Academic Publishers, 1990.

, and Boris A. Litvinskij. *History of Civilizations of Central Asia. 2, The Development of Sedentary and Nomadic Civilizations : 700 B.C. to A.D. 250*. Paris: UNESCO Publ, 1996.

Daryaee, Touraj. *The Oxford Handbook of Iranian History*. Oxford: Oxford University Press, 2012.

DeVries, Keith , Peter Ian Kuniholm, G. Kenneth, and Sams & Mary M. Voigt. "New dates for Iron Age Gordion." *Antiquity.* June 2003. http://www.antiquity.ac.uk/projgall/devries296/ (accessed August 7, 2010).

Diakonoff, I.M. "Media I: The Medes and their Neighbours." In *Cambridge History of Iran, 2, ed*, by Ilya Gershevitch, 36-148. Cambridge : Cambridge University Press, 1985.

Dietz, Otto Edzard. *Encyclopaedia of Assyriology and Near Eastern Archaeology (RLA) - Volume 9*. Berlin: W. de Gruyter , 2001.

Drews, Robert. *Early Riders: The Beginning of Mounted Warfare in Asia and Europe*. New York: Routledge, 2004.

Eadie, John W. "The Development of Roman Mailed Cavalry." *The Journal of Roman Studies , Vol. 57, No. 1/2*, 1967: 161-173.

Ebeling, Erich, and Bruno Meissner. *Reallexikon Der Assyriologie Und Vorderasiatischen Archaologie* . Berlin: Walter De Gruyter, 1987.

Ed., Appian. Horace White. *The Foreign Wars.* New York: THE MACMILLAN COMPANY, 1899.

Eduljee, K. E. ""Parsa, Persia. Page 2. Early Achaemenian History, Parsumash, Parsamash, Parsa. c 700-560 BCE." *Heritage Institute - Corporate Governance, Institutional Governance.* 2007. http://www.heritageinstitute.com/zoroastrianism/achaemenian/page2.htm (accessed April 14, 2011).

Edwards, Sean J.A. *Swarming On The Battlefield: Past, Present, And Future.* Santa Monica: Rand Corporation, 2000.

Eiddon, Iorwerth and Stephen Edwards. *The Cambridge ancient history, Volume 3, Part 1.* Cambridge: Cambridge University Press, 1969.

Euphronios, "Scythian Archer." 14 December 2007. Louvre Museum, Paris, France, http://en.wikipedia.org/wiki/File:Skythian_archer_Louvre_G106.jpg. Web, 3 Sept. 2012.

Farrokh, Kaveh. *Shadows in the Desert: Ancient Persia at War.* Oxford: Osprey Publishing, 2007.

Farrokh, Kaveh. *Shadows in the Desert: Ancient Persia at War.* Oxford: Osprey Publishing, 2009.

—. *Shadows in the Desert: Ancient Persia at War.* Oxford: Osprey Publishing, 2007.

Franks, Tommy. *American Soldier* . New York: Regan Books, 2004.

Frye, Richard N. *The History of Ancient Iran*. München: C.H. Beck, 1984.

Frye, Richard. *The Heritage of Persia*. New York: New York: New American Library; New English Library, 1966.

Fuller, John Frederick Charles. *The Generalship of Alexander the Great*. New York and Washington D.C.: Da Capo Press, 2004.

Gabriel, Richard A. *Soldiers' Lives through History - The Ancient World* . New York: Greenwood Press, 2006.

—. *The Great Armies of Antiquity*. Westport, CT: Praeger Publishers, 2002.

—. *The Military History of Ancient Israel*. Westport: Praeger, 2003.

Gabriel, Richard. *The Military History of Ancient Israel*. Westport: Praeger, 2003.

Gankovskiĭ, IUrii Vladimirovich. *The Peoples of Pakistan: An Ethnic History*. Lahore: People's Pub. House, 1971.

Gershevitch, Ilya. *The Cambridge History of Iran, Volume 2: The Median and Achaememian Periods*. Cambridge: Cambridge University Press, 1985.

Ghirshman, Roman. *Iran from the earliest times to the Islamic conquest*. Baltimore: Penguin Books, 1961.

Glassner, Jean, and Benjamin Foster. *Mesopotamian Chronicles*. USA: Society of Biblical Literature, 2004.

Green, Peter. *Alexander to Actium: The Historical Evolution of the Hellenistic Age*. University of California Press, 1993.

Haley, Thomas J. Berndt, William O. *Handbook of Toxicology*. New York: Hemisphere Publishing Corporation, 1987.

Hamilton, Edith. *Mythology*. Boston: Little Brown and Company, 1942.

Hatzigeorgiou, Karen J. "Assyrian Soldiers." 2012. http://karenswhimsy.com/assyrians.shtm. Web. 3 Sept. 2012.

Hawkins, John David. *Corpus of Hieroglyphic Luwian Inscriptions: Inscriptions of the Iron Age (Untersuchungen Zur Indogermanischen Sprach- Und Kulturwissenschaft, N.F., 8.1) (Three Volume Set)*. Berlin: Walter De Gruyter, 2000.

Healy, Mark, and Angus McBride. *The Ancient Assyrians*. Oxford: Osprey Publishing, 1992.

―――, and Edward C. Echols. *Herodian of Antioch's History of the Roman Empire From the Death of Marcus Aurelius to the Accession of Gordian III*. Berkeley, Ca: University of California Press, 1961.

Herodotus. *The Histories*. New York: Everyman's Library, 1997.

—. *The Histories*.

Herodotus, translated by George Rawlinson, edited by Hugh Bowden. *The Histories*. London: Everyman, 1997.

Hildinger, Erik. *Warriors of the Steppe: A Military History of Central Asia 500 B.C. to 1700 A.D.* New York and Washington D.C.: Da Capo Press, 2001.

Hirth, Friedrich. *China and the Roman Orient Researches into their Ancient and Mediaeval Relations as Represented in Old Chinese Records*. New York: Paragon Book Reprint Corp, 1966.

Hoffmeyer, Ada Bruhn de. " Introduction to the History of the European Sword." *Gladius Vol 1*, 1961: 30-75.

Hoffner, Harry A. Beckman, A. *Letters from the Hittite Kingdom*. Atlanta, GA: Society of Biblical Literature, 2009.

Holloway, Steven. *Assur Is King! Assur Is King!* Leiden: Brill Academic Publishers, 2002.

Holt, Frank Lee. *Thundering Zeus: The Making of Hellenistic Bactria* . Berkeley Calif: Univ. of California Press, 1999.

Ivantchik, Askold I. *Les Cimmeriens au Proche-Orient*. Switzerland: Vandenhoeck & Ruprecht, 1993.

Jacobson, Esther. *The Art of the Scythians: The Interpenetration of Cultures at the Edge of the Hellenic World (Handbook of Oriental*

Studies, Vol 2). Koninklijke Brill NV, Leiden, The Netherlands: Brill Academic Publishers, 1995. , 1995.

Jerome. "Jerome, Chronicle." *Early Church Fathers - Additional Texts.* 2005. http://www.tertullian.org/fathers/index.htm#jeromechronicle (accessed August 5, 2010).

Jones, Strabo. ed. H. L. *The Geography of Strabo.* Cambridge, Mass: Harvard University Press, 1924.

Josephus, Flavius. *Antiquity of the Jews*.

Justin. *Epitome.*

—. *Epitome of the Philippic History of Pompeius Trogus. Translated by Rev. John Selby Watson.* London: Henry G. Bohn, York Street, Convent Garden , 1853.

Kammerer, Thomas R. *Studien zu Ritual und sozialgeschichte im Alten Orient = Studies on ritual and society in the ancient Near East : Tartuer Symposien, 1998-2004.* . Berlin: Walter De Gruyter, 2007.

Karasulas, Antony. *Mounted Archers of the Steepe 600 BC-AD 1300.* Oxford: Osprey Publishing, 2004.

Karen, Radner. *Knowledge and Power.* August 27, 2007-10. http://knp.prs.heacademy.ac.uk/essentials/royalfamily/ (accessed September 16, 2010).

Kennedy, D. L., and David Braund. *The Roman Army in the East*. Ann Arbor, MI: Journal of Roman Archaeology, 1996.

Khanam, R. *Demonology: Socio-Religious Belief of Witchcraft*. Delhi: Global Vision, 2003.

Kimball, Jeannine Davis, Vladimir A. Bashilov, and Leonid T. Yablonsky. *Nomads of the Eurasian Steppes in the Early Iron Age*. Berkeley, CA: Zinat Press, 1995.

King James Bible. Nashville: Thomas Nelson Publishers, 1998.

Knecht, Heidi. *Projectile Technology (Interdisciplinary Contributions to Archaeology)*. New York: Springer, 1997.

Kristensen, Anne. *Who were the Cimmerians, and where did they come from?* Copenhagen: Det kongelige Danske videnskabernes selskab, 1988.

Kugler, Franz Xaver. *Sternkunde und Sterndienst in Babel, vol 2*. Munster in Westfalen: Aschendorff, 1935.

Kuz'mina, Elena E. Mallory, J.P. *The Origin of the Indo-Iranians*. Leiden: Brill, 2007.

Lanfranchi, Giovanni B. Parpola, Simo. *The Correspondence of Sargon II, Part II: Letters from the Northern and Northeastern Provinces*. Helsinki: Helsinki University Press, 1990.

Layard, Sir Austen Henry. *Nineveh and Its Remains: With an account of a visit to the Chaldæan christians of Kurdistan,* and the Yezidis, or devil-worshippers; and an enquiry into ... and arts of the ancient Assyrianss. New York: D. Appleton and Company, 1858.

Leick, Gwendolyn. *Historical dictionary of Mesopotamia.* Lanham, MD: Scarecrow Press, 2003.

Leick, Gwendolyn. *Who's who in the Ancient Near East.* New York: Routledge, 1999.

Lendering, Jona . The Saka tigrakhauda relief of the eastern stairs at Persepolis. 2005. na, Amsterdam. www.livius.org. Web. 3 Sept. 2012.

Lerner, Jeffery D. *The Impact of Seleucid Decline on the Eastern Plateau.* Stuttgart: Steiner , 1999.

Lipinski, Edward. *On the Skirts of Canaan in the Iron Age: Historical and Topographical Researches.* Leuven: Uitgeverij Peeters en Departement Oosterse Studies, 2006.

Livshits, Vladimir A. "Three New Ostraca Documents from Old Nisa." *Transoxiana.* July 24, 2004. www.transoxiana.org/Eran/Articles/livshits.html (accessed July 24, 2012).

Livy. *History of Rome by Titus Livius, books thirty-seven to the end, with the epitomes and fragments of the lost books. literally translated, with notes and illustrations, by.* William A. McDevitte. York Street, Covent Garden, London:

Henry G. Bohn. John Child and son, printers, Bungay, 1850.

Livy, translated by Henry Bettison. *Rome and the Mediterranean*. London: Penguin Classics, 1976.

Lucian. *Toxaris*.

Lucian, Herbert Augustus Strong, and John Garstang. *The Syrian Goddess Being a Translation of Lucian's De Dea Syria, with a Life of Lucian by Herbert A. Strong. Edited with Notes and an Introd. by John Garstang.* London: Constable, 1913.

Luckenbill, Daniel David. *Ancient Records of Assyria and Babylonia. Volume I: Historical Records of Assyria, from the earliest times to Sargon. Volume II: Historical Records of Assyria, from Sargon to the end.* Chicago: University Of Chicago Press, 1926. , 1926.

Lukonin, V.G. "Political, Social and Administrative Institutions: Taxes and Trade." In *Cambridge History of Iran, 3.2*, by Ehsan Yarshater, 681-746. London & New York: Cambridge University Press, 1983.

Mackenzie, Donald A. *Myths of Babylonia and Assyria:.* London: Gersham Publishing Company Limited, 2004.

Mahal Singh, Bhupinder. *Punjab: The Nomads and The Mavericks*. New Delhi: Sunbun Publishers, 2000.

Maqs, "Scythian comb. Soloha kurgan." 18 November 2005. Hermitage museum, St. Petersburg, Russia. http://en.wikipedia.org/wiki/File:Scythian_comb.jpg. Web. 3 Sept. 2012.

Maspero, G. *History of Egypt, Chaldea, Syria, Babylonia, and Assyria, Volume VIII, Part B* . London: The Grolier Society Publishers, 1903.

Maspero, G. *History of Egypt, Chaldea, Syria, Babylonia, and Assyria, Volume VIII, Part B.* London: The Grolier Society Publishers, 1903.

Mayor, Adrienne. *Greek Fire, Poison Arrows & Scorpion Bombs.* Woodstock & New York: Overlook Duckworth, 2003.

—. *Greek Fire, Poison Arrows & Scorpion Bombs: Biological and Chemical Warfare in the Ancient World.* Woodstock, NY: Overlook & Duckworth Press, 2003.

McClintock, John and James Strong. *Cyclopaedia of Biblical, Theological, and Ecclesiastical Literature* . New York: Harper & Brothers, Publishers, 1891.

McMurray, Heather. *Virtual Karak Resources Project* . 11 22, 2003. http://www.vkrp.org/studies/historical/scythian-point/Default.asp (accessed May 4, 2010).

Medvedskaya, Dandamayev M. and I. *Media Encyclopædia Iranica, Online Edition.* January 6, 2006. http://www.iranica.com/articles/media (accessed May 19, 2011).

Miller, J.Maxwell and John H. Hayes. *A History of Ancient Israel and Judah*. Philadelphia: Westminster Press, 1986.

Minns, Ellis H. *Scythians and Greeks*. New York: Biblo and Tannen, 1971.

Morgenstierne, Georg and Jacques Duchesne-Guillemin. *Monumentum Georg Morgenstierne, Issue 21 Volumes 21-22 of Acta Iranica*. Leiden: E.J. Bril, 1981.

Morkot, Robert. *Historical Dictionary of Ancient Egyptian Warfare*. Lanham, Md: Scarecrow Press, 2003.

Morris, Ian. *Why the West rules--for Now: the Patterns of History, and What They Reveal About the Future*. New York: Farrar, Straus and Giroux, 2010.

Art of War "Part 3 & 4." . Directed by David W. Padrusch. Performed by na. 2009.

Na'aman, Nadav. "Chronology and History in the Late Assyrian Empire 631-619 BC." *Zeitschrift für Assyriologie*, 1991: 81:243-267.

Neusner, Jacob. *A History of the Jews in Babylonia: The Parthian Period*. Chico, California : Schlors Press, 1984.

Ningyou, Map of the Assyrian Empire," Photograph. http://en.wikipedia.org/ http://en.wikipedia.org/wiki/File:Map_of_Assyria.png. 26 February 2006. Web, 5 Sept. 2012.

Nissinen, Martti, Robert Kriech Ritner, C. L. Seow, and Peter Machinist. *Prophets and prophecy in the ancient Near East* . Atlanta, GA: Society of Biblical Literature, 2003.

Norris, Edwin. *Assyrian Dictionary. Intended to further the study of the cuneiform inscriptions of Assyria, vol II.* Paris: Adamant Media Corporation, 2004.

Oded, Bustenay. *Mass deportations and deportees in the Neo-Assyrian Empire.* Wiesbaden: Reichert, 1979.

Olbrycht, Marek Jan. "THE EARLY REIGN OF MITHRADATES II THE GREAT IN PARTHIA." 2010: 144-158.

Olmstead, A.T. *History of Assyria.* Chicago and London: The University of Chicago Press, 1975 reprint (1923).

—. *Western Asia in the Days of Sargon of Assyria.* New York: Cornell University, 1908.

Oppenheim, A. Leo. *Ancient Mesopotamia: Portrait of a Dead Civilization.* Chicago & London: The University of Chicago Press, 1964.

Ovid. *On Facial Treatment for Ladies.*

—. *The Amores.*

Parpola, Simo. *Letters from Assyrian scholars to the kings Esarhaddon and Assurbanipal .* Repr. ed. Winona Lake, Ind: Eisenbrauns, 2007.

—. *The Correspondence of Sargon II, Part I: Letters from Assyria and the West State Archives of Assyria, Volume I*. Helsinki: Helsinki University Press, 1987.

Parpola, Simo, C. H. W. Johns, and Knut Leonard Tallqvist. *Neo-Assyrian toponyms*. Kevelaer: Butzon & Bercker, 1970.

Perrin, Plutarch (translated) by B. *Lives, XI*. Bury St Edmunds: Loeb Classical, 1994.

Pfeiffer, Robert H., and Robert Francis Harper. *State Letters of Assyria; A Transliteration and Translation of 355 Official Assyrian Letters Dating from the Sargonid Period (722-625 B.C.)*. New Haven, Conn: American oriental society, 1935.

Photius, and John Henry Freese. *The Library of Photius*. London: Society for promoting Christian knowledge, 1920.

Piotrovsky, Boris. *The Ancient Civilization of Urartu*. New York: Cowles Book Co, 1969.

Plato. *Laws*. New York: Akasha Classics, 2009.

Pliny, H. Rackham, W. H. S. Jones, and D.E. Eichholz. *The Natural History*. London: Folio Society, 2011.

Plutarch, and Robin Seager. *The Fall of the Roman Republic: Six Lives (Penguin Classics). Revised ed.* . London: Penguin Classics, 1984.

Polybius, Ian Scott-Kilvert, and F. W. Walbank. *The Rise of the Roman Empire*. Harmondsworth: Penguin, 1979.

Polybius. Evelyn S. Shuckburgh. translator. London, New York. Macmillan. 1889. Reprint Bloomington 1962. *Histories*. London, New York. : Macmillan. Reprint Bloomington, 1889. 1962.

Potts, D.T. *The Archaeology of Elam: Formation and Transformation of an Ancient Iranian State*. Cambridge: Cambridge University Press, 2004.

Potts, Daniel T. *A Companion to the Archaeology of the Ancient Near East*. Chichester, West Sussex: Wiley-Blackwell, 2012.

Poulos, Terrence. *Extreme War: The Biggest, Best, Bloodiest, and Worst in Warfare*. New York: Citadel, 2006.

Prevas, John. *Envy of the Gods: Alexander the Great's ill-fated journey across Asia* . Cambridge, Mass: Da Capo Press, 2004.

Rawlinson, George. *The Sixth Great Oriental Monarchy: Or the Geography, History & Antiquities of Parthia* . London: Longmans, Green, and Co, 1873.

Rea, Cam. *Isaac's Empire: Ancient Persia's Forgotten Identity*. Shelbyville, KY: Wasteland Press, 2009.

Redford, Donald B. *Egypt, Canaan, and Israel in Ancient Times.* Princeton, New Jersey: Princeton University Press,, 1993.

Reilly, Jim. "Osorkons, Sheshonks & Takeloths." *Displaced Dynasties.* 2000. http://www.kent.net/DisplacedDynasties/NebuchadnezzarChapter3.htm (accessed March 18, 2011).

Rice, Tamara Talbot. *The Scythians.* New York: Praeger, 1957.

Rogers, Robert. *A History of Babylonia and Assyria.* New York: The Abingdon Press, 1915.

Rollinger, Robert. "The Median 'Empire', the End of Urartu and Cyrus the Great's Campaign in 547 BC: (Nabonidus Chronicle II 16)." *Ancient West & East,* 2008: 51-65.

Rose, Charles Brian, G. Darbyshire, and Keith DeVries. *The New Chronology of Iron Age Gordion.* Philadelphia: University of Pennsylvania Museum of Archaeology and Anthropology, 2012.

Rose, Herbert Jennings. *Primitive culture in Greece.* Toronto: Methuen & Co. Ltd., 1925.

Roux, Georges. *Ancient Iraq.* Boston: Penguin, 1993.

Saggs, H.W.F. *The Might that was Assyria.* London: Sidgwick & Jackson, 1984.

Sauter, Hermann. *Studies on Kimmerier problem* . *(accessed December 23, 2010).* . February 6, 2002. http://translate.google.com/translate?hl=en&sl=de&tl=en&u=http%3A%2F%2Fwww.kimmerier.de%2Fstart.htm (accessed 12 23, 2010).

Sayce, A. H. *The Kingdom of Van (Urartu).* Cambridge: Cambridge, 1965.

Sayce, A.H. *Decipherment of Hittite Inscriptions.* London: PSBA 25, 1903.

—. *The Early History of the Hebrews.* London: Rivingtons, 1897.

Scholfield, A. F.. Aelian. *on The Characteristics of Animals.* New York: Harvard University Press, 1959.

Sergi, "Scythian Bronze Armor-Piercing Trilobated Arrowhead, ca 600-300 B.C.," Photograph. http://metaldetectingworld.com/ http://metaldetectingworld.com/06_finds_scythian_arrowhead.shtml. Web, 5 Sept. 2012.

Shabani, Riza. *The Book of Iran: A Selection of the History of Iran.* Tehran: Center for International-Cultural Studies, 2005.

Shahbazi, Shapour. "*Kaveh Farrokh » Blog Archive » Professor Shapour Shahbazi: The Parthian Army.*" *Kaveh Farrokh.* August 6, 2012. http://www.kavehfarrokh.com/heritage/professor-shapour-shahbazi-the-parthian-army/ (accessed August 19, 2012).

Shayegan, M. Rahim. *Arsacids and Sasanians: Political Ideology in Post-Hellenistic and Late Antique Persia*. Cambridge: Cambridge University Press, 2011.

Sidky, H. *The Greek Kingdom of Bactria: From Alexander to Eucratides the Great*. Lanham, Md: University Press of America, 2000.

Simpson, Gareth C. *The Defeat of Rome in the East: Crassus, The Parthians, and the Disastrous Battle of Carrhae, 53 BC*. Philadelphia: Casemate, 2008.

Sinor, Denis. *The Cambridge History of Early Inner Asia*. Cambridge: Cambridge University Press, 1990.

Slatyer, Will. *Life/Death Rhythms of Ancient Empires – Climatic Cycles Influence Rule of Dynasties*. Singapore: Trafford On Demand Pub, 2012.

Snodgrass, Anthony M. *Arms and Armor of the Greeks*. Baltimore: The John Hopkins University Press, 1998.

Starr, Ivan. *Queries to the Sungod: Divination and Politics in Sargonid Assyria (State Archives of Assyria, IV)*. . Helsinki : Helsinki University Press, 1990.

Stern, Ephraim. *Archaeology of the land of the Bible the Assyrian, Babylonian, and Persian periods, 732-332 BCE*. New York: Doubleday, 2001.

Strabo. *Geography*. Translated by W. Falconer. London: George Bell & Sons, 1903.

Sulimirski, Tadeusz. *The Sarmations*. London: Thomas & Hudson, 1970.

Sykes, Egerton, and Alan Kendall. *Who's Who in Non-Classical Mythology*. London: Routledge, 2002.

Syncellus. *In Roos, A. G. (ed.), Flavii Arriani quae exstant omnia. v.2. Scripta minora et fragmenta. Adiectae sunt tres tabulae geographicae et fragmentum Papyri 1284 Societatis Italianae*. Leipzig: Teubner, 1967.

Tadmor, Cogan M. & H. "Gyges and Ashurbanipal: a study in literary transmission." *Orientalia 46*, 1977: 65-85.

—. "The Campaigns of Sargon II of Assur." *Journal of Cuneiform Studies, vol. XII, no. 3*, 1958: 77-100.

Tanner, Stephen. *Afghanistan: A Military History from Alexander the Great to the Taliban Insurgency.* . New York and Washington D.C.: Da Capo Press, 2009.

Tertel, Hans Jürgen. *Text and Transmission: An Empirical Model for the Literary development of Old Testament Narratives*. Germany: Walter De Gruyter Inc, 1994.

Todman, Don. "Warts and the Kings of Parthia: An Ancient Representation of Hereditary Neurofibromatosis Depicted in Coins." *Journal Of The History Of The Neurosciences 17, no. 2*, April 2008: 141-146.

Toorn, K. van der, Bob Becking, and Pieter Willem van der Horst. *Dictionary of Deities and Demons in the Bible DDD.* Leiden: Bril, 1999.

Tsestkhladze, Gocha R. *Ancient Greeks West and East: edited by Gocha R. Tsetskhladze.* Leiden: Brill, 1999.

Tsetskhladze, Gocha. *Ancient West & East, Volume 3, Issue 2.* Leiden: Brill, 2004.

Tsetskhladze, Gocha R. *North Pontic Archaeology: Recent Discoveries and Studies.* Leiden: Brill, 2001.

Turner, Patricia, and Charles Russell Coulter. *Dictionary of Ancient Deities.* New York: Oxford University Press, 2001.

Underdown, Thomas, Heliodorus. Translated by Thomas Underdown. *An Aethiopian History Written in Greek by Heliodorus.* New York: AMS Press, 1967.

Van der Spek, R.J. "New Evidence from the Babylonian Astronomical Diaries concerning Seleucid and Arsacid history." *Archiv für Orientforschung 44/45,* 1997/98: 167-175.

Vanderhooft, David Stephen. *The Neo-Babylonian Empire and Babylon in the latter Prophets.* Atlanta, Ga: Scholars Press, 1999.

Virgil. *Aeneid.*

Vuks , V., and Z. Grbas . *Cavalry: the History of a Fighting Elite, 650 BC-AD 1914*. London: Cassell, 1993.

Ward, Steven R. *Immortal: A Military History of Iran and Its Armed Forces*. Washington, D.C.: Georgetown University Press, 2009.

Warry, John. *Warfare in the Classical World: War and the Ancient Civilizations of Greece and Rome*. London: Salamander Books Limited, 1998.

Wiesehofer, Josef. *Das Partherreich Und Seine Zeugnisse: The Arsacid Empire: Sources and Documentation*. Stuttgart: F. Steiner, 1998.

Wilcox, Peter, and Angus McBride. *Rome's Enemies (3): Parthians and Sassanid Persians*. Oxford: Osprey Publishing, 1986.

Wisenhofer, Josef. "From Achaemenid Imperial Order to Sasanian Diplomacy: War, Peace, and Reconciliation in Pre-Islamic Iran." In *War and Peace in the Ancient World*, by Kurt A. Raaflaub, 121-140. Malden, MA: Blackwell Pub, 2007.

Xenophon. *Anabasis*.

Yalichev, Serge. *Mercenaries of the Ancient World*. London: Constable, 1997.

Yamauchi, Edwin M. *Foes from the Northern Frontier: Invading Hordes from the Russian Steppes.* Grand Rapids, Michigan: Baker Book House, 1982.

Young, Rodney S. *The Gordion Excavations I: Three Great Early Tumuli (University Museum Monographs ; No. 43).* Cambridge: University Of Pennsylvania Museum Of Archaeology And Anthropology, 1982.

Index

A

Abdera, 151
Adbimilkutte, 75
Adrammelech, 37
Aelian, 162, 172
Ahlamu, 84, 85, 86
Ahseri, 72
Ahumilki, 75
Akhat-abisha, 23
akinakes, 151
Akkullanu, 80, 82, 84
Alexander, 123, 138, 172, 178, 179, 180, 184
Amazons, 143
Ambaris of Tabal, 23
Amurru, 80, 82, 85, 86, 87
Amytis, 114
Anati, 114
Anthesterius, 145
Aphrodite, 103, 104
Arameans, 85
Arda-Mulissu, 35, 36
Ardys, 77, 96
Argishti II
   listing
      Argishti, 37
Armenia. *See* Urartu
Arraphu, 113
Arrian, 99, 123, 138, 169

Artabanus, 182
Ascalon, 103, 104, 105
Ashdod, 21, 75
Ashur, 69, 70, 102, 113, 114, 115, 117
Ashurbanipal, 2, 6, 62, 63, 67, 68, 69, 70, 71, 72, 74, 75, 76, 77, 78, 79, 80, 83, 84, 86, 87, 90, 93, 94, 95, 96, 97, 99, 100, 101, 102, 109, 111, 121, 128
Ashurbanipal II, 6
Ashur-etil-ilani, 102
Ashur-uballit, 116, 118
Atargatis, 105

B

Babylonia, 22, 31, 32, 36, 78, 98, 110, 112, 117, 119, 122, 174
Babylonian, 13, 94, 107, 116, 118, 122, 124, 145, 156
Bagdatti of Uishdish, 18
Bartatua
   listing
      Protothyes, 45, 46, 47, 48, 49, 50, 51, 52, 99, 100
Battle of Carrhae, 136, 158, 159, 176, 180
Battle of Jaxartes, 178, 179
battle on Mt. Uaush, 10, 20, 21, 22
Bit-Hamban, 55, 56

Black Sea, 1, 16, 129, 135, 157, 158, 163, 173
body armor, 7, 132, 133, 134
Byblos, 75

C

Carchemish, 115, 116, 117
Chertomlyk, Ukraine, 148
China, 139, 140, 194
Chinese, 140
Chronicle of Jerome, 34
Cilicia, 39, 40, 68, 94, 97, 98
Cimmerians
   listing
      Cimmerian, 1, 2, 3, 5, 6, 7, 9, 10, 11, 12, 13, 14, 15, 16, 17, 19, 20, 24, 25, 26, 32, 33, 34, 35, 36, 37, 38, 41, 43, 44, 52, 54, 55, 56, 57, 58, 59, 60, 62, 67, 68, 69, 70, 71, 72, 74, 75, 76, 77, 78, 79, 80, 81, 82, 83, 85, 86, 88, 94, 95, 96, 97, 98, 99, 100, 102, 109, 110, 118, 120, 127, 128, 129, 131, 133, 135, 138, 139, 140, 143, 145, 146, 151, 157, 160
Cyaxares, 2, 98, 99, 105, 106, 110, 111, 114, 115, 118, 120, 128
Cyrus the Great, 107, 125, 145

D

Daiaukku, 18
Dakku, 43

Defense in Depth, 181
Dnieper-Bug estuary, 158
Dugdammi
   listing
      Tugdammi, 2, 78, 79, 80, 82, 83, 84, 86, 87, 88, 89, 90, 91, 92, 93, 94, 95, 96, 97, 98, 99, 100, 106, 108, 109, 110, 111, 128
Dur-Illil, 54, 55

E

Egypt, 67, 74, 75, 78, 101, 102, 103, 109, 113, 115, 116, 117, 121
Egyptians, 62, 102, 103, 112, 115, 116, 117
Elam, 61, 78, 81, 98
Elamite, 139
Enarees, 103, 104
Esarhaddon, 1, 10, 26, 33, 35, 36, 37, 38, 40, 41, 42, 43, 45, 46, 47, 48, 49, 50, 51, 52, 53, 54, 55, 56, 57, 58, 59, 60, 61, 62, 63, 64, 65, 68, 99, 100, 109, 121, 123, 156
Eshpai, 24
Espai. *See* Eshpai
Euphrates River, 85, 112, 114, 118
Eusebius, 34

F

Fall of Nineveh Chronicle, 2, 82, 106, 107, 118
feinting, 127, 176, 178, 179, 180

Female sickness, 104

G

Gamir, 8, 13, 15, 16, 17, 19, 20, 21, 40, 41
Gaugamela, 138
Gerrhus River, 135
Gordion, 35, 64, 121
gorytus, 163
Gutium, 45, 79, 88
Gyges of Lydia, 67

H

Halys River, 108
Harran, 62, 115, 116, 117
helmet, 138, 139, 140, 142, 169
Hercules, 150, 156, 157
Herodotus, 2, 16, 45, 48, 57, 62, 65, 66, 99, 100, 101, 102, 103, 104, 105, 106, 108, 109, 119, 123, 124, 125, 128, 132, 135, 143, 145, 146, 149, 150, 167, 169, 170, 171, 173, 175, 181, 184
Hindanu, 112
Hubushna
   listing
      Khubusna, 39, 40

I

Ionia, 94, 97
Ishpaka, 41, 42, 45, 46

J

javelin, 7, 19, 21, 143, 148, 151
Josiah, 101, 116, 117

K

Karibtu, 59, 60, 61
Kastariti
   listing
      Phraortes, 48, 57, 58, 59, 60, 61, 62
Kerch, Ukraine, 145
Kilman. *See* Kuluman
King Darius of Persia, 62, 175
King Ullusunu of Mannea, 18
Kingdom of Urartu
   listing
      Urartu, 5, 16, 20, 37, 42, 108
Kisir Gimirai, 10
Kuban River, 138
Kuluman, 25

L

Lake Urmia, 17, 29, 32, 46
lance, 129, 136, 145, 146
Lucian, 124, 150, 171
Lydia, 68, 69, 70, 71, 77, 79, 94, 95, 97, 109
Lydians. *See* Lydia

M

Madyes
   listing

Madys, 2, 98, 99, 100, 101, 106, 108, 109, 110, 111
Madys, 97, 98
Mamitiaršu, 57, 58, 59
Mannaean, 11
  listing
    Mannae, 18, 20
Mannaeans, 42, 72, 74, *See* Mannaean
Mannai. *See* Mannaean
Mannea. *See* Mannaean
Massagetae Scythians, 143, 145
Media
  listing
    Medes, 6, 7, 36, 38, 59, 64, 78, 80, 100, 105, 116, 119, 120, 125, 128
Memphis, 67
Metatti of Zikirtu, 18
Midas, 22, 23, 24, 33, 34, 35
Milkiashapa, 75
Mizraim, 75
Mugallu, 70, 71, 87, 89
Musarkisus, 7
Musur, 70, 74, 75, 76, 77

N

Nabonidus Chronicle, 107, 108, 125
Nabopolassar, 107, 112, 113, 114, 115, 116, 117, 119
Naqi'a-Zakuta, 67
Naram-Sin, 83
Nebuchadnezzar, 114, 118, 156
Necho I, 67
Necho II, 115, 116, 117

Nineveh, 2, 42, 56, 68, 70, 72, 73, 82, 91, 106, 107, 114, 115, 118, 169, 181

O

Olbia, 158
Ovid, 104, 124, 163, 173

P

Palestine, 101, 102, 103, 105, 109
Parsumaš, 55, 56
Pazyryk, Russia, 157
Pharnuches, 178
Philistia, 101
Phoenician, 75
Plato, 156, 171
Plutarch, 34, 64, 136, 167, 169, 173, 177, 179, 184
Psammetichus, 101, 115
Pseudo-Aristotle, 161, 172

Q

Qablinu, 112

R

Royal Scythians, 135
Rusa, 11, 12, 17, 18, 20, 22, 36, 37, 38
Rusa II, 36, 37, 38

S

sagaris, 143
Sakiz, 46, 52

Sandaksatru, 93, 98
Sardes, 94, 97
Sargon II, 1, 5, 8, 10, 11, 12, 13, 28, 31, 32, 33, 37, 38, 47, 64, 119, 127
Scythians
   listing
      Scythian, 2, 5, 8, 37, 38, 41, 45, 46, 47, 48, 49, 50, 56, 62, 71, 72, 78, 79, 84, 93, 99, 100, 102, 103, 105, 106, 109, 110, 111, 124, 127, 128, 129, 132, 133, 134, 135, 136, 137, 138, 139, 140, 143, 145, 149, 152, 156, 157, 158, 159, 160, 161, 163, 165, 167, 174, 175, 177, 178, 179
Sennacherib, 13, 25, 26, 33, 35, 36, 37, 38, 64, 65
Šerua-etirat, 48
Sharezer, 37
shield, 135, 149, 167
Sidon, 75
Sin-ahi-usur, 10, 19, 20, 21
Sinsharishkun, 102
Siriš, 53, 54
Strabo, 33, 64, 94, 97, 99, 121, 123, 128, 157, 162, 173
Suhi, 112
swarming, 127, 176, 177, 178, 179
sword, 37, 39, 94, 105, 143, 149, 150, 151, 152, 156
Syennesis, king of Tarsos, 151

T

Tabal, 23, 24, 25, 39, 68, 70, 71
Takrit, 113
Teishebaini, 38
Teushpa
   listing
      Teuspa, 38, 39, 40, 41
Tidcal, 83
Tiglath-pileser III
   listing
      Tiglath-pileser, 5, 6, 10
Tigris River, 80, 114
trilobate, 160
Tushamilki, 70, 74, 75

U

Uishdish, 8, 13, 17, 18, 20
Umman-manda, 38, 39, 80, 81, 82, 83, 93, 100, 113, 114, 115, 116, 117, 118, 120, 128
Urartu. *See* Kingdom of Urartu
ussi, son of Dugdammi, 87, 88, 89, 90

V

Virgil, 148, 170

X

Xenophon, 143, 151, 170, 171
Xerxes, 151

Z

Zagros Mountains, 42, 56, 72, 79, 119

Zumua, 72